THE ART OF EVANGELISM

Evangelism carefully crafted into the life of the Local Church

By

Professor William J. Abraham, D. Phil. (Oxon),
Perkins School of Theology,
Southern Methodist University.

CLIFF COLLEGE PUBLISHING
CALVER, SHEFFIELD S30 1XG Tel: BASLOW (0246) 582321

Originally published as Method in Evangelism
The Council on Church Revitalisation and Extension
Texas U.S.A. © 1988 William J. Abraham

This Revised British Edition
© 1993 Cliff College Publishing

All rights reserved. No part of this publication may be
reproduced, stored in a retrieval system, or
transmitted, in any form or by any means,
electronic, mechanical, photocopying, recording
or otherwise, without the prior
written permission of the publishers.

Cliff College Publishing,
Calver, Sheffield. S30 1XG

Printed by Loader Jackson Printers,
Arlesey, Bedfordshire

ISBN 1 898362 00 9

Acknowledgements

The writing of this book would not have been possible without the help and encouragement of a host of people. I would like to record here my debt to Bishop Ernest Dixon and the members of the Southwest Texas Conference. They gave me an unparalleled opportunity to develop this material in conversation with them. Their commitment to the renewal of the church has been a source of great inspiration.

I especially want to thank Dr. Claus Rohlfs and his colleagues on the Council for Church Revitalization for their support. More than anyone, Dr. Rohlfs has kept me on course in my efforts to bring this material to completion.

I also want to thank my wife, Muriel, and my three children, Timothy, Siobhan, and Shaun, for their constant love and help.

All thanks be to God,
Who scatters abroad,
Throughout every place,
By the least of His servants,
His saviour of grace.
Who the victory gave,
The praise let him have
For the work he hath done:
All honour and glory to Jesus alone!

His Spirit revives
His work in our lives,
His wonders of grace,
So mightily wrought in the primitive days.
O that all might now know
His tokens below,
Our Saviour confess,
And embrace the glad tidings
of pardon and peace.

Thou Saviour of all,
Effectually call
The sinners that stray;
And let a nation be born in a day!
Then, then let it spread
Thy knowledge and dread,
Till the earth is o'erflowed,
And the universe filled with the glory of God.

FOREWORD

William (Billy) Abraham is Irish and a Methodist minister. He is an academic, a theologian/philosopher with a passion for evangelism. He is Professor of Evangelism and Professor of Philosophy of Religion at Perkins School of Theology in Dallas, Texas. His previous book, The Logic of Evangelism, was a bestseller, and inspired very many. This new book finds ways in which the principles of evangelism may be put into practice. It is intended for individual reading or for groups, and has discussion questions. The aim is to help those who use it to develop a deep vision about what evangelism is, to take full responsibility for it, and to find concrete ways to express the vision in evangelism. It isn't a detailed programme of evangelism, but it provides a solid grounding on which evangelistic strategy can be built.

Abraham seeks to set out the position adopted by John Wesley, and then to show how the Methodist Church is astonishingly well equipped to be effective in evangelism. The author looks at various models of evangelism, commending particularly that of initiation into the Kingdom of God. He deals with the question of the content of the Gospel, and how both ordained and lay people play their part in sharing the good news. But he also looks at the importance of baptism and morality in relation to conversion and asks serious questions about basic belief, spiritual gifts and spiritual disciplines.

This is not an exercise in easy evangelism. It will provoke people to deep thought, and also point forward to useful activity. The appendices include a workshop on faith sharing and some guidance on how to lead another person to faith in Christ, an outline for teaching new converts the faith, and a final set of miscellaneous suggestions to help us on our way.

It's a good straightforward read on a topic of vital interest, written with a background of scholarship and a foreground of deep passion about communicating the Gospel to others. I commend it most warmly.

Donald English

Table of Contents

PREFACE

EVANGELISM WITH INTEGRITY

The material presented in this book represents a first attempt to provide local churches with a study guide which will help them develop a coherent and responsible approach to evangelism.

I take it for granted that this is a crying need in the Methodist Church. For too long we have left evangelism as a fringe activity to be relegated to the sidelines of the church's ministry. Although there is much on the current scene in evangelism which deserves our support and applause, we are all aware that many of those in the public eye who are identified with the cause of evangelism have done much to bring it into disrepute. It is understandable that many want to pass by on the other side and leave evangelism to those few good samaritans who have the nerve to pick it up and attend to it.

THE CHALLENGE OF EVANGELISM

It is my considered judgement that the mainline churches should respond to the current problems in evangelism not by turning further away from it but by redeeming it and then restoring it to a position of honour within the total ministry of the church. I think that the prospects for this within the Methodist tradition are extremely good. As I suggest in the opening chapter, Methodists have an astonishingly rich set of resources to deploy in the revitalization of this crucial ministry.

The renewal which is needed in this area will not happen, however, by chance or by accident. It will require patient endeavour and self-critical reflection over the span of a whole generation. If we want to see substantial improvement, we must be ready to take a long term view of our endeavours. Those who want a quick, easy solution are destined to experience sorrow and disillusion. We must be prepared for the kind of

7

fundamental renewal which will require of us sweat, tears, and persistent prayer. It will demand of us not just creativity and innovation of a practical nature; it will demand something of a theological revolution in our thinking.

THE UNITY OF KNOWLEDGE AND VITAL PIETY

The material developed here is the product of many years of wrestling with the challenge of evangelism both as a pastor and as a scholar. I am not interested in impractical speculation about evangelism. Nor am I satisfied to jump in the deep end and just hope for the best. I am concerned to explore the demands of evangelism in an intellectually rigorous fashion, yet to do so from within the practical ministry of the church. So what is provided here is the fruit of my work as both pastor and professor. Throughout I want to fulfil Wesley's plea to unite knowledge and vital piety.

The style is simple and straightforward. I have excluded all the trappings which go with conventional academic writing. For those who want a more developed and scholarly account of what is presented here they can consult my book The Logic of Evangelism (Grand Rapids: Eerdmans, 1989). There they will find the sources and arguments which provide the warrants for the proposals laid out here. In this volume I present my basic proposals in a popular and accessible form.

HOW TO USE THIS BOOK

The ideal way to use this book is to go through it in a housegroup or a special series of classes devoted to evangelism. It might also be used in retreat settings where committees of evangelism have sufficient time to spend a few days together. At the very least, each chapter will need a full session if the material is to be covered. There is in fact enough material in each chapter to last for at least two sessions, but I feel that there is merit in moving more quickly through the whole of the project. My primary concern is that those who use this material do three things:

1.   That they develop a deep vision as to what evangelism should be in their local situation.

2. That they own this vision fully and completely for themselves, taking full responsibility for its content and implementation.

3. That they find concrete ways to express their vision for evangelism in workable forms of ministry in their local situation.

To this end it is vital that all those involved in the use of this book, especially those who will provide leadership in its use, will take the time and trouble to think through carefully and comprehensively what is argued and suggested. This will involve not only a close reading of the text and some reflection on its content but a fair amount of thinking and reading outside the boundaries of this book in some of the reading listed at the end of each chapter. At the end of each chapter I have also provided a list of questions which naturally arise given what I have suggested earlier. The last question at the end of each chapter is extremely important. Groups should not proceed to the next chapter until it has been covered and the exact answer recorded.

EVANGELISM AND REVITALIZATION

It is my hope that this book might, by the grace of God, have some small role in the wider renewal of the church which is currently under way among us. I am excited by the signs of new life which I encounter again and again within the Methodist Church and elsewhere within Christendom. It is not naive to hope that we might yet see a major religious awakening which would equip God's people to serve Christ in his work in the world. This cannot take place without the unceasing presence of the Holy Spirit. Yet we might still dare to hope that the Holy Spirit will use our consecrated efforts to achieve God's purposes for God's people.

Note again that my fundamental concern is the development of an adequate vision of evangelism for the future. I do not outline here a detailed program of evangelism. Suggestions relevant to this will be made as we proceed but primarily I am seeking to help local congregations think through their own approach to evangelism and then to encourage them to put in place a variety of workshops, seminars, retreats, Sunday School sessions, and the like, which will together make up a vital ministry of evangelism geared to their needs.

There are two assumptions behind this approach to evangelism. First, Methodists are people who like to think and let think. They rightly want intellectual and spiritual space to think things through for themselves. Within this horizon they need the means to come to terms with the fundamental questions about evangelism which trouble them. Until we provide this, we will not get very far in establishing a responsible ministry of evangelism which we will be able to embrace and sustain over the years. Secondly, the development of an adequate ministry of evangelism needs in part to be left to those on the ground who will implement such a programme. I am confident that if this material is used properly it will lead to forms of evangelistic ministry which will stand the test of time. We need initially to sort out our fundamental principles and to be encouraged to put these into practice. This is the primary goal of this book.

CHAPTER ONE

METHODISM AND THE FUTURE OF EVANGELISM

THE FUTURE OF THE METHODIST CHURCH

The Methodist Church can have a strategic role in evangelisation over the next generation.

Many Methodists find this difficult to believe; perhaps some of them do not even want to believe it. Yet I am convinced it is true. The evidence for this is derived from a variety of sources. In what follows I want to lay out that evidence as succinctly as possible.

As we begin this task it is crucial to realise at the outset that evangelism depends first and foremost on the work of the Holy Spirit. This is the surest ground for optimism about the future of evangelism in Methodism or anywhere else. Our thinking must begin at this point.

JOHN WESLEY AND THE WORK OF THE HOLY SPIRIT

Wesley himself and his collaborators were well aware of this fact. To their surprise they found themselves as part of a movement which arose when the Holy Spirit invaded and flooded their lives. Sometimes the Spirit came like a mighty wind and quite literally swept people off their feet. At other times the Spirit came like a gentle dew; people woke up in the morning and they knew that God had met with them and changed them. Yet at other times the Spirit was like a fire which burned within them as they heard the good tidings of the gospel. Francis Asbury, one of the pioneers of Methodism in the U.S.A., puts this graphically when he speaks of having a melting time with the people in the presence of the Lord; this was his way of acknowledging a radical dependence on the Holy Spirit in the work of evangelism to which he was called. We might add that the Irish who started Methodism in North America already knew from their own experience in the homeland that without the Spirit their work was utterly in vain.

What is astonishing about John Wesley was his approach to this whole matter of the work of the Holy Spirit in evangelism. This is best seen when we compare Wesley with Jonathan Edwards and with Charles Finney. Edwards was a contemporary of Wesley and witnessed precisely the same kind of phenomena in the Great Awakening which Wesley witnessed. Indeed Wesley read Edwards very carefully and enthusiastically recommended his writings to others. This was extremely wise for Edwards is one of the best commentators on renewal that the church has ever seen.

What emerges in Edwards' analysis of the work of God is a magnificent sense of awe and wonder before the presence of the sovereign Lord, majestic in splendour and beauty. Edwards' interests are manifold but he is especially intent to separate the gold from the dross. Hence much attention is given to determining how one is to distinguish what is a true work of the Spirit from what is a fraud. In his day, as in ours, there were many misfits around who might easily lead astray those new Christians who yearned to find an authentic faith. So Edwards set himself to understand, teach, defend, and advise. As one reads in Edwards one senses a deep Calvinism hanging like a cloud in the background. A work of God is, after all, a work of God. It is a matter of God's eternal decree that God should pour out his Spirit here rather than there, at this time rather than at that time. Even to this day those writing in the Calvinistic tradition hold that awakenings in the church are a matter of divine decree. God moves and things are transformed for a season; then it is back to business as usual. The work of God in conversion and in seasons of renewal is miraculous. It is completely a matter of divine action and election even though God will work through free human instruments when he does decide to move.

Charles Finney turned all this on its head. Almost a century after Edwards' ministry he blazed a trail through the eastern and mid-western States of North America which left thousands of converts committed to Christianity. Even today he is still a legend for thousands who take their cue from him in their approach to evangelism. His approach to evangelism was business like and humanistic. He believed, of course, that the work of the Holy Spirit was essential to evangelism. Thus he was accompanied by a brother Nash who did nothing but pray for Finney's ministry; and towards the end of his life Finney ruefully acknowledged that he had failed to give adequate emphasis to the cruciality of the work of the Spirit in his endeavours. Yet overall Finney took a very different view from that of Edwards. He insisted that awakenings or revivals were fundamentally the effects of human activity. His favourite analogy is drawn from the life of the farmer: you prepare the soil, plant the seed, turn on the hoses, and then harvest the results. Likewise in the harvesting of souls. You pray, arrange appropriate meetings, teach and preach the truth like a trial lawyer before a jury, call for decision, instruct the convert properly, and you have as a result a revival. Revivals are not miracles, they are the predictable effects of certain measures which the church puts in place in the harvesting of souls.

Wesley stands in the extreme centre between these two poles. His head is more with Edwards than it is with Finney; but his hands and feet are more with Finney than they are with Edwards.

He is too good a theologian to accept the crass kind of humanism which is lurking constantly on the surface of Finney's theology. This kind of humanism is rampant in modern fundamentalism although its advocates generally do not have the spiritual discernment to see it. Wesley knew only too well the depths of human evil and corruption, and his theology of grace did not permit him to lessen for an instant the primacy of the work of the Spirit in all authentic evangelism. Yet he knew also that the Spirit works through certain means which God has ordained. Hence he had no time with those who went in for passive religion where you just waited around like the weary Calvinist for God to send another hurricane of the Spirit in from the coast. He met this very early on in his ministry in his encounter with the Moravians and he energetically set his face against it. He insisted that the people of God must sit down together in conference, converse intelligently on the work of God, and then, inspired and led by the Holy Spirit, they must put in place those practices and traditions which best served the Holy Spirit in the renewal of creation. This meant he was an assiduous organiser, preacher, teacher, critic, letter-writer, debater, motivater, and theologian. The obvious image to illuminate this is that of a large sailing boat cast afloat in the ocean. It is no good lying tethered up in the dock, forever being fitted out with equipment. Moreover, when the boat is taken out of the dock it cannot move without the winds. So the sails must be hoisted to catch their power. And it is not enough to throw the sails up in any old fashion; they must be skilfully placed if they are to be used to maximum effect. Likewise in the work of evangelism. The church needs to be rigged out with a variety of equipment, most especially with the gospel of Jesus Christ. She must then venture out into the high seas. The sails must be unfurled with purpose and care. With those in place we can then trust the wind of the Spirit to blow upon her and animate her life with grace, direction, and love.

Part of the genius of Wesley as an evangelist was his ability to strike the kind of balance which is missing in Edwards and Finney. On the one side he relied entirely and implicitly on the Holy Spirit. On the other side he relentlessly sought out those means which would serve God in the salvation of the world. This is surely one reason why he conducted a kind of study tour of the Moravian settlements in Germany. He wanted to be in close contact with those who were on to something important in the work of God. More importantly, he expected the Holy Spirit to bless those means which were prayerfully made available in humility and faith. This is precisely what happened. The effects of it even at a distance of over two hundred and fifty years are still astonishing to those who care to examine them with sympathy.

PESSIMISM IS IMPOSSIBLE

For this reason alone one cannot ultimately be a pessimist about the future of evangelism. This is a work which depends crucially on the work of the Holy Spirit and anyone who stops to reflect on what this means cannot overturn it by pleading that our present situation is too grim or that our resources are inadequate. This is exactly what could have been said about the early church in Jerusalem. It is exactly what many thought and felt about the early Methodists. Faith, however, through the eyes of divine revelation sees the situation entirely differently for faith knows that the work of evangelism is ultimately the work of God, and God simply does not abandon his purposes to save and renew creation.

One can, of course, legitimately ask whether the Methodist Church will be used of God in the work of evangelism. Perhaps God having raised it up will enter into a judgement upon it so that it disappears off the face of the earth. Moreover, one can legitimately ask whether the Methodist Church is in a fit state to be of much use in evangelism. Perhaps Methodism is too proud and corrupt to be of much use to God in the next generation. Furthermore, one can legitimately ask whether future leaders and members of the Methodist Church will be genuinely open to the Holy Spirit in the work of evangelism. Perhaps the whole membership of the church will fall into abject apostasy rejecting the presence of God from their midst.

These are not idle enquiries. There are times when the most candid observer must admit that it is questionable whether the Methodist Church is indeed in a fit state to be used of God and whether there really is a genuine sensitivity to the living God abroad in the church. But there are two things which are certain: God is committed to the task of extending his love and rule across and through creation, and God is well able to use all sorts of institutions in this process. Even if things are as grim as some think they are, there is always the possibility of renewal. After all Methodism itself began as a renewal movement, and, although it eventually and tragically separated from its institutional parent, there is no certainty that history need repeat itself.

So I deliberately leave aside direct predictions about the future. I do not know if the Methodist Church will fulfil the predictions which its lovers and critics are making about it. I have no crystal ball which tells me that it will awaken and become the giant it could be in the purposes of God or that it is destined to slide into oblivion. These things are entirely in the hands of God.

What I find interesting and worth recording is that the Methodist Church has astonishing resources which, if genuinely placed at the disposal of the Holy Spirit, could prove to be extraordinarily fruitful in evangelism. Moreover, I am concerned to convince Methodist people and their leaders that this is really the case. My claims are not a matter of plaintive rhetoric intended to keep our spirits up for one more generation; they are intended as a blunt and realistic analysis of the way things actually are.

Yet I will venture not a prediction but a prophecy. Those parts of the Methodist Church which recover the gospel of the kingdom of God, heed the call of the Holy Spirit, and follow the suggestions which follow, need have no fear of survival in the future. Those parts which do not and simply continue business as usual have a precarious future ahead of them.

THE RESOURCES OF THE METHODIST CHURCH

We can now turn to the resources which the Methodist Church has at its disposal in the arena of evangelism. My central thesis is that the Methodist Church is exceptionally well placed to be a vital force in evangelism in the years ahead. What are the resources which can be at the disposal of God in the years ahead? The following list captures the crucial elements involved.

1. The Methodist Church has an astonishing number of churches scattered across virtually every county in the country. The physical plant available is utterly astonishing.

2. The Methodist Church's connexional system allows for the fire of God's gifts and graces to flow naturally from one part of the body to another.

3. The Methodist Church has an ever increasing body of lay people who are weary of defeatism and keen to see the church become a force for the gospel throughout the land.

4. The Methodist Church has a body of people who are yearning for a deeper level of piety and

spiritual reality. There is a real desire to grow in grace and a thirst to know the living God in many quarters.

5. The Methodist Church has a vast array of highly educated ministers who, if they stopped reacting and moved out in faith, would be astonished and surprised at what God would do through them. The vast majority of ministers are neither corrupt nor ignorant; they are sincerely desirous to serve God and the people; and they have enormous potential as leaders and agents in the kingdom of God.

6. The Methodist Church has a network of colleges across the nation with strong academic traditions and which for the most part are competent and exacting in their expectations. They are being urged to incorporate the serious study of evangelism into the curriculum; properly done this could have a profound effect both in theology and in the church at large.

7. The Methodist Church has scores of individual churches scattered throughout the land which are strong in the ministry of evangelism and which are well able to provide models and inspiration for a fresh surge of activity in this area of the church's work.

8. The Methodist Church has a magnificent theological heritage which once inspired and sustained a splendid era of responsible evangelism. That heritage is still the official theology of the church and has now been made freshly available in the work done in the commissions on doctrine and in the scholarly labours on Wesley's writings.

9. The Methodist Church has a splendid record of evangelistic activity which is lying in the records waiting to be emulated. The characteristics of evangelism as carried out by Methodists are rich and exacting.

    i.   At heart Methodists have sought to lift up Jesus Christ in the power of the Holy Spirit and in compassion and mercy.

ii. Methodists have insisted that evangelism must be incorporated into a wholistic mission which involves comprehensive care of people. Thus they have thrown themselves enthusiastically into medical care, education, welfare programmes, and the like.

iii. Methodists have insisted that the gospel must be addressed to the whole person of mind, emotion, and will.

iv. Methodists have insisted that its servants in evangelism must be accountable, and they have, therefore, built into their system safeguards against financial corruption.

v. Methodists have steadfastly refused to be sectarian. They have operated in unison with others where they can; they have sought to manifest a catholic spirit; they have tried to be the friends of all and the enemies of none.

vi. Methodists have conducted their evangelism in a mood of healthy pragmatism which recognises the need for both innovation and a therapy of good order.

vii. Methodists have refused to settle for church growth as the essence of evangelism. They have sought to make full disciples of Jesus Christ who are straining forward towards full perfection. Church growth specialists have much to say to modern Methodists but in turn Wesley can act as a healthy corrective to the church growth tradition.

viii. Methodists have creatively used the sacrament of the eucharist in evangelism, seeing it as a converting ordinance as well as a crucial means of sustaining grace.

ix. Methodists have developed a tradition of song and hymn which in some places is now the jewel of the church's worship; yet they have not been afraid to strike out and use material which speaks now in the idiom of the people.

x.   Methodists have built a system of fellowship and community groups which have been gladly taken and used to great effect in many modern churches. There is already in many places the will to redeploy this lost treasure of the past.

xi. Methodists have fostered a splendid distaste for many of the faults which have bedevilled evangelism in the last hundred years or so and which have made evangelism a disgrace to the good name of Jesus Christ. Thus they have abhorred personality cults; they have kept open books on their finances; they have been outraged by attempts to manipulate people into the kingdom of God; and they have developed a lively sense of the complexity of our individual journeys out of sin into the liberty of the children of God.

LOOKING TO THE FUTURE

As I lay out this list, I am well aware of the problems which face the Methodist Church in the field of evangelism. I am aware of low morale in many places and of the maintenance mentality which has gripped some sections of the church. I know that the art of evangelism has to be relearnt again, that the good news of the gospel has been relegated in some quarters to the back pews, and that there are those who have got carried away by important secondary issues. My claim is the modest one that several outsiders have made: there is in the Methodist Church a tremendous wellspring of potential. The Methodist Church could become a magnificent agent of the spread of God's reign across the face of the earth in the last part of this tumultuous century.

If I am correct in this, then this is a time to dream dreams and to cultivate fresh vision. Now is not a time to be cynical and downhearted, nor is it a time to look back in nostalgia and weariness. It is a time to press on into the future, to repent and turn again, and to call down the power of the Holy Spirit upon us afresh.

Renewal in evangelism will not be easy. The day is far spent and our period of probation is almost over. We cannot afford another generation of inaction. Evangelism will require of us hard work in a host of areas. Taking it with the seriousness it deserves may mean revolution for many pastors; it will involve profound intellectual and theological renovation across the face of the church; and it will mean spiritual struggle which will shake us to the foundations and drive us to much prayer and fasting.

Yet God calls us to act and to move out in compassion, faith, and hope! We need to sing again with Charles Wesley:

> All glory to God in the sky,
> And peace on earth be restored!
> O Jesus exalted on high,
> Appear our omnipotent Lord!
> Who, meanly in Bethlehem born,
> Didst stoop to redeem a lost race,
> Once more to thy creatures return,
> And reign in thy kingdom of grace.
>
> When thou in our flesh did appear,
> All nature acknowledged thy birth;
> Arose the acceptable year,
> And heaven was opened on earth;
> Receiving its Lord from above,
> The world was united to bless,
> The giver of concord and love.
> The prince and the author of peace.
>
> O wouldst thou again be made known!
> Again in thy Spirit descend,
> And set up in each of thine own
> A kingdom that never shall end.
> Thou only art able to bless,
> And make the glad nations obey,
> And bid the dire enmity cease,
> And bow the whole world to thy sway.

Come then to thy servants again,
Who long thy appearing to know;
Thy quiet and peaceable reign
In mercy establish below;
All sorrow before thee shall fly,
And anger and hatred be o'er,
And envy and malice shall die,
And discord afflict us no more.

BIBLIOGRAPHY:

William J. Abraham, The Coming Great Revival (San Francisco: Harper and Row, 1985).

Jonathan Edwards, The Great Awakening (New Haven: Yale University Press, 1972).

Charles Finney, Revival Lectures (Fleming H. Revell, n.d.).

Albert C. Outler, ed., John Wesley (New York: Oxford University Press, 1964, Part One, pp. 3-116).

Albert C. Outler, Evangelism in the Wesleyan Spirit (Nashville: Tidings, 1971).

Arthur Skevington Wood, The Burning Heart, (London: Paternoster Press, 1967)

QUESTIONS:

1. Why has the Methodist Church failed in recent years to live up to its potential in the field of evangelism?

2. How would you rate the contribution of your local church to the evangelisation of your community over the last thirty years?

3. What strengths does your local church have in the field of evangelism as it faces the future?

4. Conduct a careful study of the growth patterns in your local church over the last thirty years.

5. What has Wesley to say to us about our commitment in evangelism as a denomination?

6. In the light of your reflection what concrete steps should be taken to initiate the development of a responsible, comprehensive ministry of evangelism in your church?

CHAPTER TWO

THE OPTIONS IN EVANGELISM

THREE MODELS OF EVANGELISM

Our work in evangelism is invariably related to our basic beliefs as to what evangelism is in its essentials. Thus our efforts, plans, and programmes in evangelism are derived from the fundamental way in which we think about evangelism. Suppose, for example, we construe evangelism as the proclamation of the gospel. If we take this route, we shall focus our efforts on getting the word out to as many people as possible as efficiently as possible. Suppose, however, we interpret evangelism as growth in the numbers of the church. If we take this route, we shall bend our efforts to increase church membership as quickly as possible. It is very important, therefore, that we articulate and examine our basic approach to evangelism by reviewing the main options which have developed in the mind of the church over the generations. Initially, we want to identify three different ways of thinking about evangelism which have become familiar. We also want to evaluate these alternative ways of thinking about evangelism. How faithful are they to the gospel? Do they do justice to the way in which the best evangelists have operated? Are they really adequate if we are to do the job which is laid upon us in our day and generation?

As we set out to look at various conceptions of evangelism, it is worth remembering that the word "evangelism" got lost from the vocabulary of the church for almost fifteen hundred years. Wesley, for example, did not call himself an evangelist, and we do not find him describing his activity as evangelism. When various lives of Wesley were written in the nineteenth century, he was not referred to as an evangelist but as a revivalist. Even in the early twentieth century an evangelist is sometimes defined as a writer of one of the gospels.

The story behind the loss and recovery of the word "evangelism" is a fascinating one. Even today many people are unhappy with the word; they prefer to use the term "evangelisation" instead. What matters is not so much the words we use but how we actually conceive of that work or ministry of the church which is generally referred to as evangelism. Initially the situation can look very confusing, but when we look more deeply it is very instructive.

MODEL ONE: EVANGELISM AS WITNESS.

In this position the focus initially is very broad. Any thing the church or a member of the church does to bear witness to the Christian faith is seen as evangelism. This may take a host of forms. It may mean sharing the gospel verbally with a friend, or telling others one's own experience of Christ. It may mean being kind to a neighbour at a time of need, or helping the church run a programme for underprivileged children. It may even mean engaging in acts of justice, attempting to rid the world of oppression and structural nastiness. So long as what is done is done out of commitment to Jesus Christ, then it is an act of witness; and every act of witness, on this view, is a form of evangelism.

This means that everyone is really an evangelist, whether they know it or not. After all every one is a witness of one sort or another. They may not be a very enthusiastic witness or they may not be a very good witness, but they are still a witness nonetheless. The church's task in evangelism is to be more intentional about witness. The church needs to improve its work in the world and proclaim by its life and deeds what it believes about Jesus Christ and salvation.

There are obvious strengths in this approach to evangelism.

1. It makes evangelism something which should be natural to the Christian rather than something forced and artificial. If we are all witnesses whether we like it or not, evangelism becomes a basic part of our lives as Christians.

2. It calls the church to obedience in the world. If evangelism is represented as much by acts of

mercy and love as it is by verbal proclamation of the gospel, then the call to evangelise clearly involves us in active service of the neighbour.

3. It forces us to see that evangelism does presuppose a life of obedience to Christ; otherwise, what we say in the ministry of evangelism will be hollow and hypocritical.

There are many serious weaknesses, however, which cannot be overlooked.

1. It exaggerates what can be conveyed through acts of mercy and love alone. Acts of love and witness cannot convey the crucial content of the good news of the gospel which has been central to evangelism over the centuries. This depends crucially on a handing over of the tradition about the gospel.

2. This conception of evangelism is too often used as an excuse for inactivity in the field of evangelism. If everything we do is an act of witness, and every act of witness is a form of evangelism, then everything we do is evangelism. This invariably allows us to pretend that the church has fulfilled its obligations in evangelism when in reality it has reduced evangelism to our acts of mercy and love. No church would ever have been founded if Christians had approached evangelism in this manner.

3. This approach to evangelism is really dependent on another approach to evangelism. It gets off the ground because we sometimes say that actions speak louder than words, or we say that we need to proclaim the gospel by our lives as well as our lips. We are really using the term "proclamation" in a metaphorical sense to make our point, and we are therefore dependent on another and very different conception of evangelism.

MODEL TWO: EVANGELISM AS PROCLAMATION.

This is one of the most popular conceptions of evangelism favoured by both scholars and laity. This is partly derived from the fact that the Greek terms from which we get our words "evangelism", "evangelisation", and the like, literally mean to "proclaim". So in many contemporary Christian circles an evangelist is understood as someone who proclaims the good news of the gospel. When most people think of a model evangelist today, they automatically think of someone like Billy Graham. For years Graham has proclaimed the gospel across the great cities of the world, and it is clear that he sees his role as that of a speaker or announcer of the gospel. Moreover, when people speak of televangelists they are thinking of an evangelist as essentially a proclaimer. Indeed, many look to television as the greatest medium every devised as an instrument of evangelism and are eagerly pouring millions of dollars into this kind of ministry. Television has replaced the book and the radio as the most important medium of the spoken word so it is natural that many see it as the way ahead for evangelism. Clearly, if evangelism is confined to proclamation, then television holds the key to future work in evangelism.

There are obvious advantages to thinking of evangelism in terms of proclamation.

1. It highlights the cruciality of sharing the story of God's action in Christ with those who have never heard it or with those who have only heard oppressive fragments of the Christian message.

2. It keeps the ministry of evangelism to manageable proportions and therefore fosters accountability in this area. We can clearly decide if evangelism is taking place by asking if the gospel is being preached clearly and authentically, hence we can easily gauge whether or not we are evangelising.

3. It seeks to do justice to the scattered biblical material and comments on evangelism which we possess.

There are, however, very serious objections to limiting evangelism to proclamation, as has happened over the last hundred years or so within Protestantism.

1. When we look carefully at all the biblical material on evangelism and evangelists, it is very clear that evangelists did not confine their ministry to that of proclamation. Philip, one of the few referred to in

the New Testament as an evangelist, did not simply engage in a ministry of proclamation; he also was involved in healing and in a ministry of exorcism, and he went so far as to baptise the Ethiopian to whom he explained the significance of Christ. In the patristic era evangelists stayed long enough in one area to appoint pastors for those they led to Christ. It is artificial to confine evangelism to acts of speaking and proclamation, although proclamation is absolutely essential to the total work of the evangelist.

2. In the early church one could be sure that the proclamation of the gospel would be intimately linked to the Christian community. Those who proclaimed the gospel operated from within the church, and it was natural that those who became Christians would be incorporated into the church. This is being brought into question today by the notion of some para-church organisations. They are committed to evangelism, but set themselves up as superior to the church's traditions, sacraments, and services. Although there is much talk about follow-up and discipleship, this is mostly accidental. As a result there are hosts of "born again" Christians who do not have a clue about the teaching and content of the Christian faith. Continuing to construe evangelism as proclamation fosters this tragic development in modern Christianity.

3. The great evangelists of the past did not confine their ministry to that of proclamation. When Patrick went to Ireland, or when his monks set out to evangelise the peoples of northern Europe, they did not simply preach the gospel; they saw to it that those converted were grounded in the Christian faith. When Wesley set out to work in England and Ireland, he refused to limit his labours to that of proclamation; he insisted that those who responded to the gospel be joined to other Christians, and that they be initiated, even if in some small way, into the riches of the Christian tradition of teaching and sacrament. Conversely, those who today try to keep evangelism to

preaching end up adding to this, other elements which go far beyond proclamation. They insist on altar calls, they supply the convert with basic material on prayer, bible study, and the like, and they seek to join the enquirer to a local church. They are not able to narrow evangelism to acts of proclamation.

4. Most of those who argue that evangelism should be understood as proclamation appeal to the great commission of Matthew 28 : 18-20 to support their vision. This, however, is totally inconsistent with their position, for Matthew insists that the church must make disciples, baptise, and teach. The great commission does not confine itself to proclamation. Moreover, consider how difficult it is to heed Matthew's concerns if one were to try and attend to all of them by means of modern television. Imagine trying to baptise someone from a television screen! If evangelism is merely proclamation then we could of course evangelise through television; but there is one thing we could not do: we could not fulfil the great commission.

MODEL THREE: CHURCH GROWTH

In the last generation or so some have reacted very strongly to the confining of evangelism to proclamation and have argued that evangelism must be more intimately related to the building of local Christian communities. In part this is because they want to be more faithful to the great commission of Matthew; in part it is because they want to take into account the inescapably communal character of the Christian life. Moreover, a group of scholars, inspired by the labours of Donald McGavran, have given much attention to discovering how churches in various parts of the world have actually grown. They have then applied their insights to working out how the church might now grow in the future. A whole school of thought and action has grown up to take the message of church growth across the world. In recent days special attention has been given to the growth of gigantic churches which have sprung up in various cities. The hero in this tradition is Paul Cho who has established a church in Seoul, Korea, which has over 500,000 members. Those who study church growth do not, however, confine themselves just to the superchurches; they are also keen to examine how churches grow in small towns or in rural areas. Their aim is to gather a body of evidence which will allow the specialist scholar to discern those principles which need to be applied in any particular local situation if the church is to grow. Work in this area represents one of the most powerful influences in thinking about evangelism over the last twenty years.

There are several advantages to thinking about evangelism in the light of what has been discovered about church growth.

1. It has cut through the mists of myth and half truths which have been held for generations about evangelism. Many, for example, have held that television and radio is very effective in evangelism. In actual fact the vast majority of people who actually join a local church do so because of friendship or because of a significant relationship with someone already inside the church. Or to take another issue. Many intellectual leaders of our culture both within and without the church hold that modern people are not really winnable to the Christian faith; they hold that religion is destined to decline because of the forces of secularism. This is simply false, for even in the West large numbers will actually join a church if the church is determined to win them, and if it puts in place appropriate measures to contact them.

2. Church growth advocates have made it very clear that evangelising across cultures requires great sensitivity and skill if the job is to be done properly. Moreover, there are thousands of groups who have not yet had an opportunity to respond to the gospel by joining a local Christian community which speaks to them in their own idiom and language. There is a vast missionary task yet to be fulfilled by the modern church; no amount of talk about partnership can eradicate this fact.

3. Church growth scholars have unearthed a vast body of useful information about the growth of the

church which is vital to future work in evangelism. It has shown, for example, that the growth of Pentecostalism is in part due to factors which were part and parcel of the spread of Christianity across the Roman empire. It has established, moreover, that leadership and planning are vital to effective work in evangelism. Furthermore, it has highlighted the need to attend to the possibility of group conversion and has, therefore, challenged the tendency to think of evangelism only in terms of the conversion of individuals. All this needs to be heeded and appropriated without apology.

There are, however, serious objections to certain facets of current church growth thinking.

1. Insufficient attention is paid to the demands of the Christian gospel in initial discipleship. Where a local church is weak theologically, techniques of church growth are sometimes used to swell the numbers regardless of whether there is any serious Christian commitment. Church growth theory does not deal adequately with the beginning phase of Christian discipleship. Thus it makes a totally artificial distinction between different grades of discipleship and settles for the minimum in this arena. This simply creates very serious problems for the convert at a later stage of his or her journey.

2. Church growth advocates are often ambivalent about the work of the Holy Spirit in the ministry of evangelism. Most of its leading theoreticians are theological conservatives, so formally they agree that the work of the Holy Spirit is crucial in evangelism. In practice, however, evangelism is carried out as a thoroughly humanistic exercise where everything is driven by the criterion of what will work to increase the numbers. Even healings and signs and wonders, something which is increasingly emphasised by some church growth thinkers, are treated as a kind of technique to bring people to belief and commitment.

3. Church growth thinking has failed to tackle some of the knotty problems related to the unity of the

church. Thus in North America it has proposed that we should build churches for our kind of people. Black churches for Blacks, Asian churches for Asians and Chinese churches for Chinese. This is understandable, for many churches refuse to be open to people of a different culture or race. But this plays too easily into the hands of racists who want to keep the church segregated, and it fails to wrestle sufficiently with the unity given to us in the gospel of the kingdom of God.

MODEL FOUR: INITIATION INTO THE KINGDOM OF GOD

We have now looked at three ways of thinking about evangelism. In the rest of this chapter I want to suggest another way of conceiving of evangelism. It is helpful to approach this by noting three things which will prepare the way for my central suggestions.

First, the three definitions I outlined above do not exhaust the definitions of evangelism which are used by modern Christians. We have in fact a cluster of definitions or a family of definitions which are used to identify a specific dimension of the total mission of the church. In addition to witness, proclamation, and church growth, we need to add at least the following six notions:

CONVERTING PEOPLE TO CHRIST
THE MAKING OF DISCIPLES
WINNING SOULS
CHRISTIANISING PEOPLES OR NATIONS
INITIATING PEOPLE INTO CHRISTIANITY
CHURCH PLANTING

What this linguistic richness shows is that Christians have found it essential to use a variety of terms to do justice to the complexity of the task laid upon them in evangelism. There is an unspoken inference here that it is inadequate to limit evangelism to proclamation or to converting people to Christ, much less to restrict it to aspects of modern evangelistic practice such as revivals or altar calls. We need to lift our eyes and see the broader picture which lies before us.

Secondly, it is obvious that we have here a family of ideas which can be separated from other dimensions or definable acts of Christian ministry. Whatever way we finally construe the arena marked out by the verbs mentioned above, it can clearly be distinguished from other activities in which the church rightly engages. Thus it can be distinguished from pastoral care. It can be marked off clearly in our thinking from Christian nurture or Christian education. And it is logically distinct from Christian social action or from Christian welfare programmes. Intuitively it is very odd to confuse evangelism and the cognate verbs and nouns related to it with pastoral care or Christian education or with social action. Clearly, in an ideal situation all these will be connected to each other in the comprehensive ministry of the church, but it is muddled and confusing to collapse evangelism into any of these ministries. This is surely one reason why theologians have been forced to construe evangelism as a subject of enquiry worthy of attention in its own right. It is hopelessly inadequate to construe evangelism merely as an indirect dimension of all that we do in theological colleges.

The third point is more difficult to make but it is extraordinarily illuminating for our reflection on evangelism. It is not an accident of history that the verbs we mentioned above have been used in close connection with one another. They represent the fragmenting and shattering of a single, comprehensive vision for evangelism which I suspect gripped the early church in its ministry of evangelism. This was never formalised conceptually, but I am very tempted to believe that it was held instinctively by most of those engaged in evangelism.

The issue can be expressed sharply in this way. The area marked out by our scattered verbs represents those fundamental actions and goals of the church related to entry into, and grounding, in the dynamic reign of God inaugurated in the life, death, and resurrection of Jesus Christ. This provides the crucial clue to what the church has been about when it has sought to evangelise. In its evangelism it has intentionally sought to initiate people into the gracious rule of God which has descended upon us in mystery and unimaginable grace in Jesus Christ through the ministry of the Holy Spirit. The goal of evangelism is to ground, establish, institute, and train people in the reality of God's rule. That rule was made manifest in Christ, it is offered in all its penultimate fulness to the Christian church since Pentecost, and it already strains for fulfilment in the parousia of the risen Lord. More prosaically we might say that the task that faces us in the modern church is to rebuild the porch of entry into the kingdom of God by retrieving the good news of God's decisive acts of inauguration in Christ and by providing appropriate initiation into the fulness of God's reign in creation and history.

We can express this now by means of a simple definition. EVANGELISM IS BEST CONSTRUED AS THAT SET OF ACTIONS WHICH ARE GOVERNED BY THE INTENTION TO INITIATE PEOPLE INTO THE KINGDOM OF GOD.

What this means in practice is that evangelism embraces a variety of actions all held together by the single intention to initiate people into the reign of God's love and justice. It will mean proclaiming from the housetops the good news of the gospel. It will require the inviting of people to repentance and faith. It will lay upon us the task of bringing people to the waters of baptism and into genuine relationship with the Christian community. It will mean leading people into a relationship with God the Father through the Son by the action of the Holy Spirit, so that they are born again into the glorious liberty of the sons and daughters of God. It will lead us to hand over the fundamental moral vision of the Christian faith summarised in the great commandment to love God and love the neighbour. It will require the handing over of the Christian intellectual heritage so magnificently summed up in the scriptural canons and creeds of the early church. It will imply the bringing of people to the broken body and blood of our Lord made known to us by the Holy Spirit in the eucharist. It will involve ensuring that people are equipped by appropriate gifts of the Holy Spirit to operate as agents of God's reign in the church and in the world. Finally it will mean introducing people to the rudiments of the spiritual disciplines such as the study of the scriptures, prayer, and fasting, so that they will be kept constantly in touch with those means of grace without which they will fall into confusion and spiritual death.

Why should we approach evangelism in this way? Let me indicate just four reasons for adopting this vision of evangelism.

1. This vision is derived from the fundamental theological horizon which meets us in the gospels. There we are confronted with the inauguration of the rule of God promised to Israel, constituted by the life, death and resurrection of Christ, and carried through in the ministry of the Holy Spirit in the early church. It is from within this horizon that we need to rebuild our theology of evangelism.

2. This vision breaks the impasse which has distracted us for so long in modern debates about evangelism, namely the debate between those who stress social action and those who stress personal evangelism. The centre of all we do in the church is neither evangelism nor social action but the coming of the rule of God into our midst. Neither evangelism nor social action can stand alone nor can they be seen as the primary horizon of the church's life and action. The first task of the church is to celebrate and worship. As we invite our sovereign, living God to be present in our midst and to rule over the new Israel, we are to raise a shout of joy in the presence of the Lord, we are to enter into songs and sacraments of love, and we are to hold weekly festivals of celebration. From this centre we reach out into the world to carry the good news and to welcome others into the fellowship of the saints and martyrs. This is the heart of evangelism. From this centre, we also reach out into the whole of creation to invite God to reign among us in justice and peace. This is the heart of Christian social action. Evangelism which does not produce agents of the kingdom of God is fruitless and bogus; social action which is not derived from the gospel of the risen Christ is rootless and ephemeral.

3. This vision represents what the great evangelists of the church have actually tried to do. From Paul in

Asia Minor to Gregory the Wonderworker in Armenia, from St. Patrick in Ireland to Cyril and Methodius in Moravia, from Matteo Ricci in China to John Wesley in England, from Mary Slessor in West Africa to Lottie Moon in Asia, in their own way all of these have sought to bring people into the fellowship of God's kingdom. We rightly honour them as models in the field of evangelism.

In modern times we have forgotten this deeper vision and reduced evangelism to narrow and inadequate proportions. Church growth theorists reduce it to sophisticated measures to increase church membership, sitting lightly to the interior responsibilities and privileges of the people of God. Conservative Evangelicals reduce it to proclamation, modelled on a rational sermon preached from an elevated Reformed pulpit. Wesleyan evangelicals reduce it to stories of personal religious experience capped off by emotional altar calls which act as substitutes for baptism and other public rites of entry into the community. Pietists reduce it to converting people to an inward religion which hangs loose to the intellectual and sacramental moorings of the church. Liberals reduce it to acts of moralistic witness which are orphaned from the lights and powers of the Holy Spirit and which are sometimes radically divorced from the gospel itself. Radicals abandon the whole thing in disgust, turning their backs ironically in the name of sociology on the institutions of the faith, yet marshalling all the political clout they can muster to further their own narrow ideological pursuits.

One is reminded of A. N. Whitehead's comment: "If man (sic) cannot live by bread alone, still less can he live off disinfectants." Charismatics reduce it to a splendid display of signs and wonders which constantly threatens to lapse into apostasy and greed. Catholics reduce it to a tidy routine of catechesis and sacrament which degenerates again and again into nominalism and hard ritualism. Television evangelists reduce it to a soap opera of trinkets, personality cults, and respectable propaganda.

To be sure, I exaggerate. Most of these traditions and movements have something entirely legitimate to contribute to the debate about evangelism. Besides, most of us are wise enough to rise above our official commitments. Happily, in examining the data, I have found that we unwittingly incorporate elements of rival models of evangelism into our ministry. The time has come, however, to gather up our fragmented and scattered approaches to evangelism and hold them together in a single vision which is rooted in God's action in Christ, sustained by the indwelling Holy Spirit, mediated to us in the church through the means of grace. I am bold enough to believe that such a vision is located in a comprehensive attempt to see ourselves and all creation initiated into the incomparable mercy and love of God which is to be found in our entry into the kingdom of God. Working this through in practice could well be the key to the renewal for which we all both hope and pray.

4. Finally, we should heed this conception of evangelism because it just may have half a chance of matching the context in which the church must currently operate. To speak personally, I have been driven in this direction as much by my experience of pastoral and evangelistic work in modern Ireland as from interaction with the biblical sources and the tradition of the church. Expressing the issue quite bluntly, I have found in my experience in Ireland that we live in a world which will not be converted to Christ and nurtured in genuine holiness if it reduces evangelism to church growth, to moral activism, to verbal proclamation, or to signs and wonders. Thankfully no one really reduces evangelism to these alone, for, by the grace of God, our practice generally outshines and corrects our theology. We know instinctively that we must press for full initiation into the kingdom of God if we are to hold out for the best. We live in a world where people are

addicted to drugs, to greed, to racism, to terrorism, and to a host of sins which will not be tackled without the fulness of the reign of God in our midst. The gospel will not make progress without the presence of righteousness, peace, and joy in the Holy Spirit. What is needed is not just more talk, or more programmes of church growth and evangelism, but the mysterious power of the Holy Spirit present both in our hearts and blowing afresh in our worship, in our proclamation, and in our deeds. Moreover, we need the skill and the boldness to incorporate the new disciple into the full privileges and responsibilities of the kingdom of God. Anything short of this will be ultimately ineffective and ephemeral. It will fail to build the church of Jesus Christ, it will not enable new Christians to withstand the ravages of the modern world, and it will fall drastically short of the precious promises handed down to us in scripture, in our memory, and in the tradition given to us by our fathers and mothers in the faith.

We would do well to claim with John Wesley our birthright in the gospel.

Spirit of Grace, and health, and power,
Fountain of light and love below,
Abroad they healing influence shower,
O'er all the nations let it flow.

Inflame our hearts with perfect love,
In us the work of faith fulfil;
So not heaven's host shall swifter move
Than we on earth to do they will.

Blessing and honour, praise and love,
Co-equal, co-eternal Three,
In earth below, and heaven above,
By all thy works be paid to Thee.

Thrice Holy! Thine the kingdom is,
The power omnipotent is Thine;
And when created nature dies,
Thy never-ceasing glories shine.

BIBLIOGRAPHY:

William J. Abraham,   The Logic of Evangelism
    (Grand Rapids: Eerdmans, 1989), chaps. 2,3,4.

Mortimer Arias,   Announcing the Reign of God
    (Philadelphia: Fortress Press, 19xx).

Emilio Castro,   Sent Free
    (Grand Rapids: Eerdmans, 1985).

Michael Green,   Evangelism in the Early Church
    (Grand Rapids: Eerdmans, 1970).

George G. Hunter III, To Spread the Power
    (Nashville: Abingdon, 1987).

John Wimber,   Power Evangelism
    (San Francisco: Harper and Row, 1986).

QUESTIONS:

1. Who are your heros and heroines in the field of evangelism? What do you most dislike in the practice of evangelism?

2. How would you define evangelism?

3. How does evangelism differ from Christian education? How does it differ from social action?

4. Which vision of evangelism outlined above best describes your church's view of evangelism in recent years?

5. Which vision of evangelism do you prefer? Why?

6. What does the great commission of Matthew 28:18-20 say to us about the nature of evangelism?

7. In the light of your deliberations what concrete steps should be taken in the ministry of evangelism in your situation?

CHAPTER THREE

THE GOSPEL

GETTING THE STORY STRAIGHT

How are we to summarise the heart of the Christian gospel? This represents one of the most important questions which we must face in evangelism. Most of those whom the church seeks to reach are like the Irish woman who was chatting a neighbour over the fence in her backyard; She wanted to know just two things: "Who did it?" and "Did he get caught?"

There are two dangers to be faced. The first is to say too little and thus distort the message. The second is to say too much and lose the listener. The really great evangelists strike the right balance for their situation.

Consider D. L. Moody. When Moody went to England and Scotland he had enormous success in bringing people to Christ. Yet he was a layman; he had virtually no formal education; and you could put most of his theology on a postcard. Crowds flocked to hear him. When he went to London he preached in one of the leading churches in the city. At the end of his sermon he asked people to stand if they wanted to become Christians. So many stood that he asked them to sit down so that he could explain a second time what they were doing. The second time around they still stood up in response. Many have concluded from this that the essence of evangelism is to take the simple message of Moody and tell it just like he did.

They are correct to stress the importance of summarising the message simply. They are wrong in insisting that this was all there was to the success of Moody. Moody succeeded in part because he was speaking to people who were already steeped in the Christian faith. In Scotland he spoke to thousands who had been taught a catechism which laid out the great themes of the Reformation. Those who heard Moody had also come to believe that salvation was entirely a work of God; all they could do was wait passively in the hope that God might have elected them and would in his own good time save them. When Moody marched among them with his American accent and his heart of love and told them that they could be saved here and now, this was astonishing to them. Burdens rolled off their backs; the relief that came to them as they came to repentance and faith was entirely natural.

Our present situation is completely different. People have not been exposed to a systematic presentation of the Christian message. Church members have picked up only fragments of the Christian tradition. Many of them have made decisions and come forward to the altar, yet they are confused about what this means. They came forward hoping to feel something mysterious in their hearts, but they have little idea of how this is connected to the gospel of the kingdom of God. Even theological students and ministers are confused. They have been exposed to so many competing interpretations of the Christian message that they scarcely trust anyone, least of all themselves, to get the message straight. Currently Christian communities are bombarded with books and tapes which lead ordinary people to swing between moods of hope and despair in their quest for the essence of the gospel.

Wesley is instructive on this issue. On the one hand, he was a scholar who could acquit himself fairly well in the world of learning; he taught logic and Greek at Oxford. On the other hand, he was a popular evangelist; he could preach effectively to thousands of miners at five o'clock in the morning as they went to work. In his situation he had to summarise the faith with integrity and then follow up with forms of teaching and discipline which would establish the new convert in the faith. This was a staggering achievement which took years to develop and perfect.

In this chapter I want to address the question of what the gospel is. The church which is confused about this will fail in evangelism. I shall suggest that the heart of the gospel is the coming of the reign of God in Jesus Christ. We need both a longer and shorter version of this if we are to make much progress. Absolutely every church member should be clear about these matters.

CURRENT SUMMARIES OF THE GOSPEL

Before we proceed to this, however, it is helpful to pause and note some of the summaries of the gospel with which we are all familiar.

1. For some the heart of the gospel is the message that Jesus has come to bring us self-esteem and peace of mind.

In this perspective the focus is on the loneliness and brokenness of people who are cut loose from friendship and from genuine community. The good news is that God loves each individual; this is manifested for all to see in Christ. God desires now to give each of us happiness and contentment; we should reach out in trust and accept ourselves as God has accepted us. This done, we can build dreams of assurance and hope for ourselves. Conversion in this tradition means that we should come to love and respect ourselves, accept the love that God has for us, and attempt to share that love with others.

2. For some the essence of the gospel is that Jesus has come to save us from hell and damnation.

In this perspective the emphasis in the good news is that we can be saved from the disaster that awaits us in the life to come if we have not repented and come to Christ. This is often set in a context where the emphasis is on various tribulations and raptures which are to befall us at the end of history. The favoured biblical book is the book of Revelation. God is seen as the great cosmic judge who has sent Christ to bear the punishment which we deserve because of our sins. If we do not accept Christ, then we will be lost for ever. The good news is that if we repent and accept Christ, we can have eternal life in the age to come. Conversion, on this view, is seen as a turning to Christ in order to secure a place in heaven when we die.

3. For some the soul of the gospel is that God has come to liberate us from oppression and political bondage.

This way of thinking about the gospel has become popular in the last ten years or so. According to this position the essence of the gospel is that God is at work in history to liberate the poor and the oppressed from bondage and suffering. The favourite biblical text is the story of the exodus where God breaks the power of bondage and sets the children of Israel free. The oppression from which we are liberated is seen in a variety of ways. Sometimes the emphasis is on liberation from capitalism or from poverty; sometimes the focus is on freedom from dictatorship; at other times liberation is seen liberation from racism, sexism, or classism. Conversion in this tradition is understood as a turning to a life of social transformation where the structures of society are radically changed; if need be, this can take the form of violent revolution.

4. For some the kernel of the gospel is that God desires to bring us health and wealth.

This understanding of the gospel has gained enormous ground both in the West and in the Third world. The key to the message is that God is a good God who wants his people to prosper. God wants to give us all abundant life. God does not want his people to be sick; they can be healed now through the activity of the Holy Spirit. Nor does God want his children to travel second class; God wants his people to be successful in business and in life generally. The good news is that through Christ and faith in his word we can prosper here and now. Conversion in this perspective involves turning to Christ, trusting in the word of faith, and giving generously to the ministry of those who brought the good news of prosperity. Giving money is seen as a seed which will be returned many times over in riches and blessing by God.

There is no need to go into the strengths and weaknesses of these attempts to set forth the essentials of the gospel. Nor am I claiming that these alternatives are mutually exclusive. Clearly they overlap, and one often finds them stitched together haphazardly in a single sermon. I see the same fundamental problems in all of these ways of presenting the heart of the gospel.

1. The primary emphasis is on us and on what we need. Either we need to be affirmed, or we need to be saved from eternal damnation, or we need to be released from oppression, or we need to be healed and given success in life. Consequently God and God's actions are interpreted as taking us out of the trouble in which we find ourselves. This whole orientation breeds a shallow and superficial understanding of the Christian message. All these alternatives focus on ourselves and our needs.

2. What God has done in Christ is strictly a means to an end in these various schemes. If Jesus did not bring us self-esteem, or if he did not save us from hell, or if he did not support our social and political crusades, or if he did not bring us health and wealth, then he would not be worth attending to or following, much less worshipping and loving. There is no sense in any of these alternatives that Jesus Christ is intrinsically attractive and sovereign.

3. The good news of the gospel in all of these summaries is hopelessly narrow and reduced. It does not connect in any deep way with God's action in creation, with the depths of the human predicament, with the sweep of God's action in ancient Israel and now in the church, or with the depths of God's purposes as those shall be revealed in the future. What has happened is that a fragment here and there of the Christian message, or perhaps an implication for our conduct drawn from it, has been picked up and erected into the heart of the gospel. As a consequence those converted under these messages are often spiritually crippled and malformed.

THE HEART OF THE GOSPEL

How might we spell out the heart of the Christian gospel so that it genuinely captures the fulness of the good news? We need to do two things at this point. First, we need an overview of the Christian message. I shall provide this by developing a brief outline of the Christian faith in everyday language. Secondly, we need to focus on the substance of what Christ came to do in the world. Expressed at its sharpest Christ came to bring the kingdom of God into our midst and thus to save the world from sin and slavery.

AN OVERVIEW OF THE CHRISTIAN MESSAGE

The Christian faith can be summed up accurately in the following six points.

1. *Background beliefs about creation*. The everyday world we live in is here because of the creative activity of God. It is not a mere accident which just happens to exist; it is not the creation of a committee of gods; it is the effect of the activity of the one true God who is almighty, utterly ingenious, unreservedly good, and the unadulterated expression in his inner being of unconditional love.

2. *Convictions about the uniqueness of human beings*. The world is astonishingly rich and diverse in character. Centuries of study and research still leave a host of questions unanswered. Yet within creation human beings are unique for they are made in the image of God; they are spiritual agents made to relate to God in harmony and union. They are not just trousered apes; they are not just a particular mixture of physics and chemistry topped off by an astonishing computer in the upper part of their bodies; they are uniquely personal agents like God in their capacity for thought, moral deliberation, and spiritual relationships. Their ultimate welfare depends on their relationship with God; they live suspended between life and death, depending on how they respond to God.

3. *A diagnosis about what has gone wrong with the world*. Clearly something has gone amiss with the

world. It is not what it ought to be. The fundamental reason for the mess in which we find ourselves is that we have rebelled against the boundaries of our created existence, rejected God from God's rightful place in the universe, and become sinners. The problem is not in social structures, in a lack of education, in a failure of nerve, and the like; it lies in the depths of our souls where we are estranged from the true roots of our existence so that our fundamental relationships are out of joint. Because of our alienation from God we live in a world of illusion and half-truth, we harbour deep distrust of God, and we are paradoxically bent on our own destruction. We know radical evil in our souls.

4. *A prescription about the solution to our ills.* The fundamental solution to our predicament of alienation and distrust is to be found in the action of God. God has never left us without a witness, however much we may have perverted that witness. Moreover, God has acted decisively in Israel and in Jesus Christ to establish his rule of justice and mercy in creation. While sustaining the universe and working providentially in history to achieve his purposes, God has come to us in his eternal Son and lived among us; God has taken our rebellion into his own bodily existence and triumphed over death and destruction in the resurrection. All those who have welcomed the light of God's saving action are joined together in the Israel of God; they are equipped by God's Holy Spirit to show forth the love of God in their lives and to act as agents of the kingdom of God in the world. The solution on the human side is found in turning to the offer of God's renewal, living in deep trust in God, and venturing forth on a life of obedience to Christ in his church. The problem is so deep within us that all this is only made possible through the mysterious work of the Holy Spirit. So the resolution of our dilemma is not found in some scheme of self-help, some pro-gramme of revolutionary reconstruction, some system of education, and the like. These fail

because they are ultimately shallow and superficial. We need to be made holy and divine, and this is something only God can do.

5. *A vision about the future*. A start has been made on the renewal of creation but it awaits its full flowering. The reign of God has been inaugurated in Jesus Christ who was crucified, is now risen from the dead, and shall return in glory to bring God's purposes for creation to fulfilment. Therefore schemes of evil and madness are now obsolete and out of date; they are destined to be surpassed in the final great and terrible Day of the Lord when God's kingdom shall be fully established in heaven and earth. On the one hand, this generates a deep sense of hope for God's good purposes for creation will triumph; evil will not have the last word; love will win in the end. On the other hand, it inspires a sense of awe, for we know that we shall stand before the judge of all the earth and give an account of our actions.

6. *A vision for living*. All this generates a very particular way of living which touches every aspect of our lives. We are to live as mirrors of God's nature and thus manifest in our lives the love which God is in his triune being from eternity to eternity. We gladly love God with all our hearts, souls, and minds, and we love our neighbour as ourselves. This is the heart of the Christian ethic and its shape and precise character has been spelled out in the scriptures, in the tradition of the church, and in the lives of the saints. Our lives are not ruled by utility, or by expediency, or by reason alone. Our minds are caught up in the renewal of creation made possible by the work of the Holy Spirit.

This particular rendering of the Christian faith could be spelled out much more fully. Over the years the church has elaborated on aspects of it; again and again numerous Christian thinkers have expressed its central elements with flair and elegance. It is kept alive in part because it is constantly under challenge. The issues addressed here cannot be escaped. Every person has a kind of informal answer to the questions which are dealt with above. We all have convictions about creation; we entertain some notions about what makes human beings different from the rest of creation; we stop and think now and then of why we are in the mess that we are in; we have some idea about what needs to be done to put things right; we hold to some kind of vision of the future; and we have some idea about how we ought to live if we are to find fulfilment. In our society we are constantly bombarded by competing accounts of these issues. We are engaged in a market of philosophies which jostle to win our allegiance.

Across the generations we see this in the alternatives laid out by the great religions of the world. These have always been accompanied by a host of cults and sects who have sought to sell us their brand of salvation. In our contemporary situation these have been joined by several secular worldviews which seek to win us to their faith. Marxists and humanists, for example, seek to convince us that our destiny and happiness is to be found in a radical rejection of religion and in turning to a bold use of our own resources to solve our problems. These claims are embedded in wider visions of reality which can be spelled out along the lines we mentioned above. Perhaps the most attractive option which currently confronts us is in the West is a form of hedonism. This invites us to find our true welfare in an endless round of pleasure and happiness. Human beings are depicted as happiness machines who can be satisfied at will if the right dose of materialism and greed is administered. The proponents of this view take great care not to raise any deep questions about the origins of our life and destiny. They assume that we got here somehow, and they take for granted that life is bounded by birth and death. They do not mind if God and religion are brought into the picture so long as they do not interfere too drastically with our pursuit of the good life on earth. They suggest that what has gone wrong is that people have not given enough attention to their own needs; we have spent too long paying attention to the emotional and moral dandruff of others. Their solution to our ills is to invite us to enjoy ourselves to the full and not worry about the future. The future is unknown; tomorrow we may die; let us therefore live for today. Of course, we can never manage this if we are stupid and fail to meet some of the expectations laid upon us by others; but we should keep these to the bare minimum and look out for ourselves.

In the light of these alternatives it is crucial that we grasp the internal logic of the Christian faith. We do not need to present all of it as we present the gospel to others but we need to understand what is at stake. There is a genuine battle for the mind in the world which Christians need to understand. Otherwise they will fail to understand the real significance of Jesus Christ and present the good news of the kingdom of God in a shallow way. In fact, I suspect that many people have never really heard the good news of the gospel. They have been confronted with broken fragments which have held out exaggerated hopes and spurious promises. As a result the church in the West is itself in desperate need of the gospel.

THE GOSPEL IN A NUTSHELL

The only thing that the church eventually has to offer is Jesus Christ.

In Jesus Christ we have the eternal Son of God incarnate in our midst; he has come in incomparable love and mercy to bring in the reign of God which has been cast aside from the beginning of creation. That reign was manifest in his speech and action. He taught us the fulness of the mystery of the kingdom of God; he made manifest the kingdom in his ministry of exorcism and healing. His own life was the full embodiment of the reign of God in history. He took upon himself the evil and chaos of the world in his crucifixion, suffering for us in atonement. God raised him from the dead and vindicated his ministry. The risen Lord sent the Holy Spirit to his followers who have become his body and agents in the world. That body is equipped to continue Christ's ministry of salvation to the ends of the earth. It enters into celebration of God's mighty acts of salvation and in hope strains towards the final unveiling of the kingdom of God. Jesus Christ, crucified, risen, and coming again is the heart of the good news.

As a consequence of the drawing near of the reign of God, the church calls on the world to repent and believe. We are to have a radical change of heart and mind; we are to ponder what God has done; we are to enter into the kingdom of God in faith and joy, gladly owning its full responsibilities and privileges.. Only by doing so will we find our true destiny and fulfilment. This path will involve suffering and struggle; but it will ultimately make us like God and bring us to eternal life itself. Our response and renewal in all of this is only made possible by the activity of the Holy Spirit who reveals to us the living Christ and raises us up to new life in the kingdom.

Notice several things about the substance of the gospel.

1. The gospel is centrally the good news of God's action in Jesus Christ. It is this that we are called to announce to the whole creation.

   The message is not directly about ourselves. Thus it is not a string of stories about our personal experiences, nor a tissue of moral maxims designed to win friends and influence people, nor a revolutionary harangue about how to establish utopia in the next generation. The gospel is not a soothing talk on how to find happiness and self-esteem. The message is fundamentally a piece of good news about a slice of history which embodies the story of God's sovereign acts to break the power of evil and inaugurate his rule. That has happened once and for all in Jesus Christ, and it continues now through the work of the Holy Spirit in the body of Christ.

2. The gospel is fundamentally an astonishing and extraordinary story.

   The message is not a speculative philosophy held together by a set of rickety arguments. The gospel is not a set of esoteric secrets on how to get health and wealth. Nor is it a recipe on how to be decent and on how to become a member of the middle class. The good news is basically a narrative about the action of God in Jesus Christ. The whole thing stands and falls by the truthfulness of the witness to the cross and resurrection. It claims that the immortal God has died as our saviour to rescue us from death and bondage, to bring us as his children into his kingdom, and to establish us as the firstfruits of the new creation.

3.   This gospel is intrinsically attractive as it stands. The message needs no public relations firm or advertising agency to make its content look good.

Once the church tries to apologise for it, or tries to improve on its content by clever means and devices, then the church has lost faith in the gospel. It is as if a man were to recommend the beauty of the woman he loves by chattering endlessly about the car she drives or the clothes she wears. Anything we might roll out to make Jesus Christ look good will never match what we have in him. We cannot appeal to the lesser to support the greater. There simply can be nothing greater than the reality of God's involvement in history to save the world. Once we lose this we have really lost the heart of the Christian faith and taken to offering lesser gospels. As Jesus taught us, once people taste what the kingdom of God is like they will sell all they have to get more. Stumbling across it is like finding treasure in a field and then getting rid of everything else to obtain that treasure.

With this in place we can now begin to develop a comprehensive approach to evangelism. Our first task is to let God's rule come in the worship of the living God in the church. We might refer to this as the raising of a thousand tongues to sing. Our second task is to find ways and means to spread the good news to people where they are. We might refer to this as the recovery of the trumpet voice in the world. Our third and final task is to put in place means of initiation into the kingdom of God which shall see people grounded in the reign of God on earth. We might refer to this as the rebuilding of the door and the porch of the kingdom.

BIBLIOGRAPHY:

William J. Abraham,   The Logic of Evangelism
            (Grand Rapids: Eerdmans, 1989), chap 1.)
Mortimer Arias,   Announcing the Reign of God
            (Philadelphia: Fortress Press, 1985).
Theodore Stylianopoulos,   The Gospel of Christ
(Brookline, Massachusetts: Hellenic College Press, 1981).
John R. W. Stott,   The Contemporary Christian
                (Leicester: IVP, 1992)
C. S. Lewis,   Mere Christianity
            (New York : Macmillan, 1964).
John Wesley, "A Plain Account of Genuine Christianity,"
in Albert Outler, ed.,   John Wesley
 (New York: Oxford University Press, 1964), pp.181-196.

QUESTIONS:

1. What was your understanding of the gospel as you came to faith?

2. How would you summarise the gospel now?

3. What is the kingdom of God? How is it related to the gospel?

4. How well does your congregation as a whole understand the substance of the Christian gospel?

5. Where do you see weak and sub-christian accounts of the Christian gospel in contemporary forms of evangelism?

6. Can you think of ways in which Christians obscure the intrinsic attraction and truth of Jesus Christ?

7. What concrete steps should be taken by your congregation to implement the issues covered in your deliberations?

CHAPTER FOUR

SHARING THE GOSPEL

We looked in the last chapter at the message entrusted to the church of Jesus Christ as it seeks to be an agent of evangelism in the modern world. It is imperative that the church get its message straight and that it has the courage to share it with the world. We are under a clear mandate to take the gospel to the ends of the earth. We must not be distracted by confused believers, by theologians alienated from the church, by hostile opponents, or by idle Christians. All Christians are summoned to play their part in this process. How are we to do this? In this chapter I want to identify some of the crucial avenues which Christians can use to share the gospel. My aim is not to be exhaustive. I want to stimulate my readers to think through what they might do in their situation under the guidance of the Holy Spirit. Bear in mind that this is just one step in the total process of evangelism.

THE ROLE OF THE CLERGY IN PROCLAMATION.

Ordained ministers have a critical role in the sharing of the gospel. They set the tone of a local congregation as teachers, administrators, advisers, and agents of encouragement. They can often make or break the evangelistic ministry of a church.

One of their crucial responsibilities is in the area of evangelistic preaching. There are two possibilities worth pursuing here.

a. Ministers should develop the art of relating the gospel to the central themes of their regular preaching. This is by no means easy. I once knew a leading Australian Anglican minister who had learned over the years to finish every sermon on an evangelistic note. This required great discipline and care for it is always easy to throw in a few lines about the cross or the kingdom in the last few minutes of a sermon. Some ministers preach nothing but evangelistic sermons and thus abandon their ordination vows to teach the flock of Christ. Others never preach an evangelistic sermon and thereby also fall into sin. Combining the two is an art which needs careful cultivation. Those who work with the lectionary may well find this a way to enrich their evangelistic efforts in preaching.

b. Ministers should prepare and preach specifically evangelistic sermons setting forth the good news of the kingdom with a view to inviting the hearer into the kingdom of God. I would advise ministers at this point to take steps to make this a vital part of their regular ministry. Initially they may be scared to do this. If they persevere, the rewards are tremendous. Here are a few suggestions which may prove helpful.

i. Ministers should take time to examine some of the sermons preached by the evangelistic giants. They could well start with the Wesleys and move to people like Charles Finney, D. L. Moody, E. Stanley Jones, Clovis Chappell, Martyn Lloyd-Jones, John Stott and Arthur Skevington Wood. It is helpful to gather a body of material so that one will have a variety of models from which to work. In time one will be able to take a text and begin to think through how Wesley would have preached it, or Chappell, or whoever else one finds helpful. We need to foster a commitment to excellence by examining what has been done in the past with care. You might find it useful to join with a group of other preachers and pool resources. Comparing notes on evangelistic preaching could be invaluable.

Note that the aim throughout evangelistic preaching is determined by the goal of initiating people into the kingdom of God. The aim is not to make the preacher or hearer feel better, or to swell the numbers of the church, or to further some political interest, or the like. The aim here is not even to get people to come forward to the altar. The aim is to provide a clear account of what the gospel is, so that those listening really understand what it is, and so that they may freely and gladly enter into the kingdom of God, accepting both its demands and its privileges. This should be kept in mind at all times. There must be real substance in what is said. Decisions to enter into the kingdom must be related to the full truth of the gospel. Too much evangelistic preaching has been thin in content and far too focused on our response to the truth rather than the truth itself. Everything that needs to be said should be said in the sermon rather than tacked on in an emotional appeal at the end.

ii.   Let preachers take some time to prepare an evangelistic sermon on some of the great evangelistic texts of scripture. Obvious possibilities in this regard are texts like John 3:16, Ephesians 2:8, Romans 8:16, Mark 1:15, and the like. There are hosts of texts from which to choose. At the beginning of this process it may be necessary to double the preparation one would normally take. Then the prepared material should be preached with flair, seeking the anointing of the Holy Spirit. There are many people within our church who have never really heard the gospel clearly and winsomely; preachers should set themselves to change this for good.

This could be usefully combined with the holding of a regular guest Sunday when the whole congregation would invite friends and neighbours to church on a particular Sunday. The whole liturgy could then be organised with this in view. Various churches have tried this with great success.

THE ROLE OF THE LAITY IN PROCLAMATION.

Preaching evangelistic sermons within church buildings is part of the remedial work that has to be done in the modern church. It is essential because we have abandoned evangelism and allowed nominal Christianity to flourish among us. Moreover, it is helpful because some outsiders will come to church to find out about the content Christianity. Yet if this is the only avenue of sharing the gospel we have at once disobeyed Christ and failed to reach people where they are. The vast majority of people are won to the kingdom of God through contact with Christians who have shared the faith with them by word and deed. Spreading the gospel through networks of relationships and friendship is central to evangelism.

It is absolutely essential, therefore, that Christians find a way to share their faith with others on a regular basis. Two kinds of sharing should be identified.

a. The first mode is the sharing of the content of the good news of the Christian message. Here the focus is on the objective content of what God has done to reclaim the world through Jesus Christ.

Each Christian should be able at this point to provide a brief outline of the gospel message which is both true to the New Testament and which is expressed in his or her own words. In chapter three I provided one such outline.

b. The second mode is the sharing of one's own personal journey of faith. Here the focus is on one's own response to the gospel. In some circles this kind of sharing takes the form of a personal testimony. One tells in simple language how one came to faith in Jesus Christ. This may have happened slowly and naturally within a Christian home and within the family of the church, or it may have happened more dramatically in a more conscious conversion experience.

Again, each Christian should be able to provide a realistic and brief account of one's own journey. They should also have the skill to share this with friends without apology or embarrassment. Properly done, this can also have a profound effect in a regular evangelistic service or on other appropriate occasions in the life of the church.

This kind of skill cannot be picked up from a book on evangelism. The best way to proceed is for the church to provide workshops on faith sharing which will tackle both possibilities. This should then be followed up by developing a system of accountability which will provide encouragement and feedback to those who are sharing their faith on a regular basis with others. A small nucleus within the church could well do the workshops and set up accountability groups themselves. A list of material for following up on this is given at the end of this chapter.

OTHER POSSIBILITIES FOR SHARING THE FAITH.

If clergy and laity together set about the sharing of the faith in the ways specified above then the church will have gone a long way to fulfilling its responsibilities in the announcing of the good news. There are other avenues for proclamation which can usefully be pursued, however.

a. One such avenue is an extended period of evangelistic preaching by someone skilled in the proclamation of the good news of the kingdom. Sometimes this has been accomplished in seasons of revival meetings but there is deep confusion in the modern church about the purpose of these meetings. There is a place for a series of meetings which focus specifically on the proclamation of the gospel to the outsider. This is one way to reach out to the whole community in a concerted effort. Such a series of meetings needs to be thought out from start to finish. It will not do to roll out the traditional revival meeting. The whole series of meetings needs to be geared to the reaching of the outsider and the preaching, music, and format should be related thereto.

b. Another avenue is to arrange visitation teams to follow up visitors, or to call systematically on every home in a designated area. This will require extended training but the effects can be extensive. There are a variety of programmes to follow; the most widely used is that of Service

Evangelism developed by Richard Armstrong and that of Evangelism Explosion developed by James Kennedy and more recently Good News Down the Street by Michael Wooderson.

c. Another avenue is to make available good Christian literature to friends and neighbours. The writings of C.S. Lewis has been very helpful to many. Biographies of people like John Wesley or Augustine's <u>Confessions</u> can be given away free. We need to make use of the wealth of material written by those who have found health and salvation in Jesus Christ. Each local church should develop a list of books which have helped members understand the essentials of Christianity. Some of these could be distributed systematically to homes in the neighbourhood of the church or placed in public places where people can have access to them.

d. In some places a local church can share the gospel through the standard channels of modern media. Those with access to local newspapers, radio, television, and the like, can use these to announce the kingdom. This will take imagination and flair but talent for this can sometimes be found within our churches. I have heard recently of a Methodist minister with a radio ministry to police officers. He had been a police officer before entering seminary and had creatively hit on this as one way to reach his former colleagues.

e. At some point a local church should examine carefully how it might reach out to those that are hard to reach. There are various groups outside the church: there are, for example, drop-outs, left-outs, locked-outs, and opt-outs. A strategy which will reach one group may have no impact on another group. Those responsible for evangelism should periodically review the whole ministry of evangelism with this in view. Over time a congregation should develop a variety of ways of sharing the faith which will touch the whole spectrum of human need and temperament.

BIBLIOGRAPHY:

Michael Green,   Evangelism in the Early Church
           (Grand Rapids: Eerdmans, 1973).

H. Eddie Fox and George E. Morris,   Faith-Sharing
           (Nashville: Discipleship Resources, 1986).

Richard Armstrong,   Service Evangelism
           (Philadelphia: Westminster Press, 1979).

D. James Kennedy,   Evangelism Explosion
           (Wheaton: Tyndale House, 1977).

G. Howard Mellor (ed.),   The Good News Works
           *(London: Home Mission Division of the
           Methodist Church, 1992)*

Michael Green,   Evangelism through the Local Church
           (London: Hodder, 1990)

Michael Wooderson,   Good News Down the Street
           (Grove Booklet)

Michael Wooderson,   Good News Down Our Street
           (London, MARC, 1991)

John Finney,   Finding Faith Today,
           (Swindon: Bible Society, 1992)

Graham Horsley,   One Plus One, A Practical
           Guide to Faith Sharing,
           (London: Home Mission Division, 1992)

Grove Booklets on Evangelism
           (Bramcote, Nottingham, NG9 3OJ)

Sermons

John Wesley,   Sermons

John Wesley, Trans into Mod English, James D. Holway,
           Sermons on Several Occasions

Arthur Skevington Wood,   For All Seasons
           (London: Hodder 1979)

Grove Booklets on Evangelism
           (Bramcote, Nottingham, NG9 3OJ)

QUESTIONS:

1. What is the role of clergy in evangelism?

2. What can a congregation do to enhance the evangelistic ministry of its pastor?

3. How far is the gospel being proclaimed on a regular basis from the pulpit of your church? What can be done to improve your present situation? How can your local church foster excellence in evangelistic preaching without neglecting the office of teaching?

4. Develop the blueprint for a weekend workshop which would equip a group of laity to share their faith with others. Provide a detailed outline of the whole weekend, showing the sessions plans, the goals of each session, the content of each session, the expected outcome, follow-up events, and the like.

5. What is your church doing to equip people to share the gospel with others in their everyday life? What needs to be done to put things right for the future?

6. What special strategies should your church develop to be effective in proclaiming the gospel in your community? Are there avenues which are currently neglected which need to be restored or which should be created from scratch?

CHAPTER FIVE

CONVERSION, BAPTISM & MORALITY

MOVING BEYOND PROCLAMATION

The great evangelists of the past did not confine their evangelistic activity merely to the sharing of the good news of Jesus Christ. They were also concerned to see people firmly established in the kingdom of God on earth. They may not have described their work in exactly this fashion, but this is a plausible way to interpret their activity.

I argued explicitly for this view in the second chapter of this book. My claim is that all we do in evangelism should be guided by the intention to bring people into the reign of God on earth. Our Methodist heritage has taken this with the utmost seriousness. The early Methodists, both itinerant preacher and local member, were constantly on the lookout for those who were already responding to the good news of the kingdom. They were not content to share the message or their testimonies and leave it at that. They were intent on fostering the development of genuine disciples who were on full stretch for all that God had offered in the gospel. This is one of the unique features of evangelism in the Methodist tradition. It has enormous possibilities for the future.

The issue can be raised in an acute form if we ask the question: What is the church going to do with those who show an interest in the good news of the kingdom of God? Do we just open the doors, fill the pews, and leave it at that? Such a policy may save our institutions, but it will not do justice to what the Lord requires of us. Nor will it begin to satisfy those who have tasted the joys of the kingdom of God. Wesley graphically summarised the issue when he suggested that there is a door and a porch which we all have to walk through if we are to enter into the kingdom of God. In other words, there is a many-sided process which we can identify when we reflect on entry into the kingdom of God.

METHOD IN EVANGELISM

I suggest that there are six dimensions to entry into the rule of God.

1. A MORAL dimension.

   Entry into the kingdom of God involves a receiving of the substance of the Christian moral tradition summed up in the great commandment to love God and our neighbour.

2. An EXPERIENTIAL dimension.

   Entry into the kingdom of God involves an experience of conversion or new birth wherein our sins are forgiven and we enter into a covenant relationship with God.

3. A THEOLOGICAL dimension.

   Entry into the kingdom of God involves a receiving of the Christian intellectual heritage summed up in the ecumenical creeds of the early church.

4. A HORIZONTAL dimension.

   Entry into the kingdom of God involves entering into the church of Jesus Christ in baptism and confirmation, joining ourselves to the saints and martyrs of the ages.

5. An OPERATIONAL dimension.

   Entry into the kingdom of God involves committing ourselves to work as agents of the kingdom in the world, equipped by the Holy Spirit to do the works of the kingdom.

6. A DISCIPLINARY dimension.

   Entry into the kingdom of God involves a receiving of the classical disciplines of the Christian life represented by prayer, fasting, and a regular use of the means of grace.

In order to help us remember these six dimension I have used an acrostic. The first letters of the key words describing the six dimensions of initiation spell out the word METHOD. When I speak of putting method back into our evangelism, I mean, therefore, much more than that we simply be intentional about what we do in evangelism; I mean that we should incorporate these dimensions of initiation into the kingdom into the heart of our evangelistic ministries. Attending to these dimensions is the pathway to grounding people in the reign of God on earth. It is one way to do justice to the mandate of the great commission.

In my view it does not matter very much where we begin in dealing with the various dimensions of initiation. What matters is that we attend to all of these elements at some time or other. For example, many people in our culture are already committed to the Christian moral tradition. Yet these people may never have experienced the saving grace of God in their personal lives. They do not know, for example, that they can have genuine assurance of forgiveness of sins. Forgiveness surely requires attention if they are to be properly initiated into the kingdom of God. Others may know and have experienced forgiveness, but their moral lives are in chaos, or they will have nothing to do with the church. Clearly they need to be taught the rudiments of Christian morality and brought into the church if we are to be serious about their entry into the reign of God. Over the next two chapters we shall deal with the six dimensions of initiation which we have identified above. In this chapter we want to look at conversion, baptism, and the Christian moral tradition. In the next we shall look at the creed, spiritual gifts, and spiritual disciplines.

CONVERSION

When the kingdom of God comes among us through the preaching of the gospel and the work of the Holy Spirit, our lives cannot ever be the same again. The classical text which speaks to this is John 3:3. "Truly, truly, I say to you, unless one is born from above, one cannot see the kingdom of God." The imagery used here is very graphic. Talk of new birth is one way of signalling that we can genuinely begin all over again. When God's rule begins to operate in our lives, this is precisely what happens.

On the one side we are forgiven all our sins. Through the work of Christ on the cross we are forgiven once and for all. Our sins are buried in the ocean of God's mercy and love. Through faith in Christ's atoning work we are acquitted of our sins. In repentance we forsake our old ways of selfishness and enter into a new relationship with God where we find the Holy Spirit giving us assurance of pardon and forgiveness.

On the other side the Holy Spirit brings about a genuine change in our lives. We are born again into the kingdom. The analogy underlying this is very compelling; Wesley used it with great skill. He suggested that outside the kingdom of God, our lives are marked by darkness and ignorance. We are like a baby in the womb before birth. We have ears but they do not hear the sounds of creation; we have eyes but they do not see the wonders of God's world. This applies to us spiritually. Before our new birth we may have a dim awareness of God but we live in spiritual darkness and ignorance. As we are exposed to the gospel, it acts as a midwife bringing us the light of God's salvation. The Holy Spirit opens our spiritual ears and eyes to hear and to understand the depths of God's love for us and for all creation. Hence we are born again from above and become children of God. There are several things to note about the new birth as outlined here.

First, it is intimately related to such terms as conversion, justification, and Christian assurance. This is not accidental. All these concepts hang together to provide a wonderfully thick description of the experiential dimension of our entry into the kingdom of God. Christianity is an intensely personal religion. Through the coming of Jesus Christ, we are giving the opportunity of turning around and being converted to a new way of life. Through the work of Jesus Christ on the cross we are offered forgiveness of our sins. Through the work of the Holy Spirit we are brought under conviction of sin, we are given the opportunity to start all over again, and we are given assurance that we are children of God. Our personal experience of entry into the kingdom of God is therefore complex and many-sided.

Secondly, it should not surprise us then that there is no single pattern which everyone must follow.

There are times of crisis when we may be intensely aware of what is happening; there are also times of process when radical change is taking place and yet we are totally unaware of what the Holy Spirit is doing. It is also vital that we do not attempt to impose our sequence of experience on others. This only creates confusion and resentment in those we are seeking to convert to Christ. Yet we must also draw attention to the impact of the coming of the reign of God in our personal lives. Properly interpreted and sensitively presented this brings great hope and liberty into our personal relationship with God. What matters in the end is not the pattern of our experience but the genuineness of our coming to know God personally, so that we are really aware of God's forgiveness and power in our lives. It is this that talk of conversion, justification, and new birth is meant to capture. It does this admirably when we come to terms with its full meaning.

Thirdly, it is important not to lose sight of the challenge of discourse about conversion and new birth. Some people are uneasy with this language because they feel it leaves no room for growth in the Christian life. Most Christians are painfully aware of how far they have to travel in their relationship with God; so it is natural that they shy away from language which seems to suggest that they have somehow arrived. They naturally feel that they need to be born anew every day or that they need to be born over and over again. This is understandable. We never cease growing in our relationship with God; there is always more progress to be made in our spiritual lives. Yet we must make a beginning somewhere, and we must never underestimate how decisive it is to enter into the kingdom of God. It is both a privilege and a challenge; for this reason alone we need to take very seriously the fact that entry into the kingdom involves new birth and conversion. Neither of these concepts eliminate the need for endless growth and development in our relationship with God. We need to stress the importance of both crisis and process in our relationship with God; the one without the other is inadequate and misleading.

BAPTISM

A second dimension of entry into the kingdom of God is captured in the sacrament of baptism.

The coming of the rule of God on earth creates a new community which lives in and for the kingdom. One enters into that community by baptism or by baptism and confirmation. Any account of initiation into the reign of God which ignores this social dimension of initiation is hopelessly inadequate. To express the matter sharply, one cannot say that one wants to enter into the kingdom of God but that one refuses to join the community of the kingdom, the church. The church and the kingdom are inextricably linked to each other. The kingdom of God cannot, of course, be identified with the church; yet the kingdom comes in part through the activity of the Holy Spirit working in and through the church. The church subsists within the kingdom of God and exists to serve the coming rule of God. Jesus made it very clear in choosing the twelve disciples that he intended to establish a community, the Israel of God, which was to carry the gospel to the ends of the earth and bring converts into its membership by baptism.

It is vitally important that the modern church re-establish a link between baptism and the ministry of evangelism. At one level the issue at stake is the very meaning of entry into the kingdom of God. To enter into the kingdom involves us in entry into the community of the kingdom. This is not a matter of personal choice on our part. Christianity is not a solitary religion; it is inescapably communal and social in character. So we cannot accept Christ as our Lord and Saviour with one breath and then in the next breath reject membership in the body of Christ, the church.

At another level the issue is one of spiritual survival. Young Christians will wilt and die if they are not placed in a body of believers who regularly participate in the means of grace given to the church. This was one reason why Wesley established the class meetings in Methodism. At a very basic level they helped instruct the new believer in the rudiments of the Christian religion, and they provided mechanisms of nurture and healing for those who were growing in grace.

At a third level, what is at stake is the service of the Christian in the world. Christian are placed in the body of Christ that they might be his hands and feet here and now. They cannot adequately serve Christ if they are living lonely, isolated lives, disconnected from other parts of the body.

In the history of the church baptism has become rich in symbolism. It has signified the washing away of our guilt and our sins through the work of Christ in the cross. It has acted as a symbol of the new birth, indicating our need to make a fresh start when we encounter the reign of God through the work of the Holy Spirit. It has served to draw attention to our need to be buried with Christ in his death and rise again with Christ in his resurrection. It has been used to signify our entry into the church, the body of Christ. It has acted as a form of witness to the world that we have joined ourselves to Christ and his body. And it has also served as a means of confirming our commitment to follow Christ in obedience to his will. There is no need to draw very tight boundaries around the significance of baptism; it is an event rich in meaning and has served perfectly adequately as a sacrament of entrance to the body of Christ.

There has, of course, been much debate concerning the mode and the subjects of baptism. Arguments have swirled around whether we should baptise by total immersion and whether baptism should only be administered to those who have explicitly come to repentance and faith. We cannot resolve these debates here; the discussion about these issues will continue indefinitely. Nor should all this worry us. What matters is not the mode or the exact timing of baptism. What is important is that Christians should be baptised at some point in their lives and that they be genuinely grafted into the church. There are advantages and disadvantages with both believers' baptism and with infant baptism. Those who practise believers' baptism tend to treat children as little pagans until they have sinned enough to repent; while those who practise infant baptism tend to underplay the need for personal conversion and new birth.

The Methodist Church practises infant baptism; yet it has been careful to emphasise the need for personal commitment and conversion. It holds that infants are rightly the subject of baptism, marking them from the beginning as members of the church and as subjects of the activity of the Holy Spirit. One of the reasons why Methodists practise infant baptism stems from their convictions about the priority of grace in our experience of God. We are saved and converted not because of our good thoughts and initiatives towards God but because of God's initiative towards us. We can only respond to God in the first place because God has moved towards us in mercy and grace. Without prevenient grace, that is, the grace that comes before our efforts and actions, we would never come to enter into the kingdom of God. Infant baptism expresses this in a very powerful way.

Yet we do need to respond ourselves to the grace of God. Hence, in order to take seriously the personal side of decision and commitment, it has been the custom over the years to hold confirmation classes for those who have been baptised as infants. This is the Methodist way of insisting that entry into the church calls for personal decision and conversion on the part of its members. It is also a way of giving each of us the opportunity to opt out of Christianity altogether should we so decide. That is one reason why in confirmation classes we attend to what it means to be a follower of Christ in some detail. It highlights the content of Christian discipleship and the need for genuine personal commitment.

There is no reason why this pattern of baptism-confirmation cannot be integrated into a comprehensive pattern of initiation into the kingdom of God. There may be a need for substantial reform in certain places, especially where baptism and confirmation have become empty rites, divorced from the gospel and the work of the Holy Spirit. But each local church will have to decide this for itself. What is absolutely crucial is that entry into the church become an inescapable part of the spiritual journey of those who are invited to enter into the kingdom of God. The natural place for this to be expressed is through baptism and confirmation. A way must be found in each local context to forge a very clear link between evangelism and baptism.

The link between the two is supplied by the fact that baptism is one dimension of our entry into the kingdom of God. Christian initiation is fundamentally initiation into the rule of God; it is not just initiation into the church. Yet Christian initiation cannot leave out or ignore initiation into the church for this is essential to full initiation into the kingdom. Baptism needs, therefore, to be placed alongside conversion as essential to entry into the kingdom. Perhaps Jesus said as much in John 3:5: "Unless one is born *of water* and the Spirit, one cannot enter the kingdom of God."

MORALITY

A third dimension of entry into the kingdom of God is captured in the great commandment to love God with all one's heart, soul, mind, and strength, and to love one's neighbour as oneself.

This is brought to our attention in the gospels in the incident recorded in Mark 12 where a scribe asks Jesus which is the first commandment of all. Jesus answered by reciting the two commandments to love God and love one's neighbour. The scribe is well pleased with the answer. Jesus in turn is delighted with the wisdom of the scribe, and says to him: "You are not far from the kingdom of God."

It is obvious that there is a clear connection between entry into the kingdom of God and a change in moral outlook and character. To enter the kingdom of God is to embrace a particular moral tradition; that tradition is summed up in the great commandment to love God with all one's heart, mind, soul, and strength, and to love one's neighbour as oneself. Again it is important to express the issue sharply: one cannot claim the blessings of the reign of God and reject the commandment to love God and love one's neighbour. Part of what it means to become a follower of Christ is to receive his moral teaching with gratitude and enthusiasm. Indeed the Christian moral teaching is not a cumbersome law imposed upon us; it is another gift of God's grace given to us for our welfare. We might also say that the Christian moral tradition summed up in the great commandment is the appropriate response to the coming of the reign of God in Jesus Christ. Given the astonishing expression of God's love made known to us in Christ, it is appropriate and natural that we should love God and that we should love those whom God loves, namely, our neighbours.

John Wesley and the early Methodists clearly understood the connection between morality and the gospel. This is explicitly spelled out in the tenor of the General Rules adopted as early as 1739. When one joined the early Methodist societies the condition of membership was very simple. All one had to do was to exhibit a sincere desire to flee from the wrath to come and to be saved from one's sins. This desire in turn would be made manifest in a moral commitment which was at once negative and positive. On the one hand, one would cease to do harm to others, refraining from evil of every kind. On the other hand, one would do all the good one could, doing good of every possible sort, and, as far as possible, to everybody. This is a sane and astute way to highlight the inner harmony between Christian experience, captured by the language of conversion and new birth, and outward behaviour, directed especially in love toward one's neighbour. Wesley was surely right to insist on this as a minimal condition of membership in the Methodist societies.

As we pursue this claim it is important to bear the following considerations in mind.

1. There is absolutely no attempt to smuggle some kind of doctrine of justification by works back into the conditions of entry into the kingdom of God. We enter the kingdom not because we have earned some kind of moral entry fee by our behaviour but because of the mercy and grace of God. As we enter the reign of God we do so acquitted by grace through faith. What is at stake here is our response to God's gracious initiative in establishing his kingdom. That response in turn is inspired by the activity of the Holy Spirit who in turning us towards the kingdom engenders within us a desire to love God and love our neighbour. In fact we come to love

God because God first loved us and because the love of God has been shed abroad in our hearts by the Holy Spirit. This explains how it is that the law of love is seen as an expression of yet more grace, given freely to us by God.

2. In focusing on the great commandment, we do not wish to exclude the vast body of ethical material handed down to us in the scriptures and in the Christian moral tradition. The scriptures of the old and new Testament are laden with ethical imperatives and moral reflection which every Christian receives with gratitude. Moreover, in the Christian moral tradition there is a unique body of ethical distinctive which are essential to the life of holiness. For example, Christians have a very particular perspective on sexual morality, on concern for the poor, on the use of violence, on the sanctity of life, and the like. Over time these are picked up and internalised by the maturing convert. What is at stake here is a simple, clear-headed summary of the heart of the Christian moral tradition. This Christ himself provides in the great commandment to love God and one's neighbour. It is this that those entering the kingdom need to grasp and lay hold of as they are initiated into the kingdom for the first time.

BIBLIOGRAPHY:

John Wesley, "The Scripture Way of Salvation,"
in Albert Outler, ed.,   John Wesley
(New York: Oxford University Press, 1964), pp. 271-282.)
-------- "Justification by Faith," ibid., pp. 198-209.
-------- "The Witness of the Spirit," ibid., pp. 209-220.
William J. Abraham,   The Logic of Evangelism
         (Grand Rapids: Eerdmans, 1989), chaps. 4, 5.
John Baillie,   Baptism and Conversion
         (London: Oxford University Press, 1964).
George Morris,   The Mystery and Meaning of
                      Christian Conversion
         (Nashville: Discipleship Resources, 1981)
Peter Toon,   About Turn
                      (London: Hodder, 1987)

QUESTIONS:

1. What is METHOD in evangelism?

2. Can you find alternative terms to designate the six dimensions of initiation into the kingdom of God mentioned above?

3. What is conversion? How would you explain the new birth to someone who had never heard of it before?

4. Can Christians be certain of their salvation? Is this important for the new convert?

5. What is the place of baptism in evangelism?

6. What is your experience of confirmation? How can it be related in a meaningful way to initiation into the kingdom of God?

7. What moral commitments should we expect of the new convert?

8. What are the General Rules of the Methodist Church? Can they serve a useful function today in the initiation of people into the reign of God?

9. What specific actions need to be taken to implement the judgements arrived at in discussing the content of this chapter?

CHAPTER SIX

CREED, SPIRITUAL GIFTS, AND SPIRITUAL DISCIPLINES

THE IMPORTANCE OF INITIATION

Over the last chapter and the present chapter we are exploring what is involved in initiation into the kingdom of God. At the beginning of the last chapter we explained very briefly the fundamental dimensions which must be covered if we are to do justice to the coming of the reign of God into our midst in Jesus Christ. We then proceeded to identify three of those dimensions. At the beginning of this chapter I want to pause and draw attention once more to the importance of initiation. We shall then proceed to deal with the last three dimensions of initiation.

One way to approach the crucial significance of initiation is by addressing an objection which can very naturally be made against the proposals I am advocating. The objection is this: In laying down these various dimensions of initiation are we not imposing a form of discipleship on the Christian convert? Surely it is sufficient to proclaim the gospel and lead people to Jesus Christ and leave it at that?

Attractive as this alternative may be initially, it fails for at least two reasons. First, the fundamental elements in initiation I am seeking to identify are integral to a deeply Christian account of the structure of our existence in the kingdom of God. The coming of the reign of God is not some vague brand of piety or religion without content. The kingdom is a very particular reality given to us in history and it was worked out in history with a particular structure and character. It has a very particular impact upon our inner lives, our relationships with others, our moral outlook, our minds, and so on. This is the case historically, as we can see in the developments which took place over the years in the early church, and it is the case in our individual lives, as we can see in the varied biographies of those who have become Christians.

Secondly, the convert needs the kind of nurture I am seeking to describe if they are to survive in the midst of competing alternatives which clearly meet us in a hostile world. Let me give a concrete example. Some years ago before I left Ireland to come to North America, I led a farm-worker to Christ. It was a kind of textbook conversion. The person concerned had been searching for God for weeks and was ripe to come to repentance and faith in Jesus Christ. It was a moving experience to see him find liberty and joy in the Holy Spirit. Two years later when I returned to visit the area, I made inquiries about Tom. I discovered two weeks after I had led him to Christ that he had been taken under the wing of a group of bigoted, political, anti-catholic Christians who proceeded to initiate him into a form of Christianity which was profoundly inadequate and deeply hostile to vital dimensions of the kingdom of God.

We are faced with stark choices at this point. We can leave the beginning Christian in a vacuum without instruction. This is like leaving newborn babies to fend for themselves without milk and food. Alternatively, we can abandon him or her to be initiated into forms of the Christian life which have next to nothing to do with the kingdom of God. This is like leaving our children to be instructed in forms of life which are barbaric and uncivilised. Or we own the need to broaden our conception of evangelism to embrace a responsible and comprehensive form of initiation. This is the only option open to us if we are to follow model evangelists like Paul or Wesley. Moreover, all of us as we embark on our journey of faith need some basic, foundational instruction and help. If the church does not attend to this, someone else will. So let us turn again to the basic dimensions of initiation we mentioned above.

CREED

The arrival of the kingdom of God led to an intellectual and theological revolution in the ancient world. The basic ingredients of that revolution were developed and splendidly expressed in the councils of the early church over a period of several centuries. They are captured in the early creeds of the church, and, in various forms, they are currently presented in the constitutional documents of the historic churches. Their content is enshrined in Historic Texts of British Methodism, the Deed of Union of the Methodist Church and the pages of the Methodist Service Book. It is imperative that this intellectual heritage be handed over in a summary form to those entering the kingdom of God.

The best known summary of the theological backbone of the Christian intellectual heritage is the Apostles' Creed.

I believe in God, the Father almighty,
creator of heaven and earth.
I believe in Jesus Christ, his only Son, our Lord.
He was conceived by the power of the Holy Spirit
and born of the Virgin Mary.
He suffered under Pontius Pilate,
was crucified, died, and was buried.
He descended to the dead.
On the third day he rose again.
He ascended into heaven,
and is seated at the right hand of the Father.
He will come again to judge the living
and the dead.
I believe in the Holy Spirit,
the holy catholic church,
the communion of saints,
the forgiveness of sins,
the resurrection of the body,
and the life everlasting.

Another summary can be found in the Nicene Creed, the only creed which has been approved by a universal council of the church.

I believe in one God, the Father Almighty, maker of heaven and earth, and of all things visible and invisible.
And in one Lord Jesus Christ, the only-begotten Son of God, begotten of his Father before all worlds, God of God, Light of Light, very God of

very God, begotten not made, being of one substance with the Father, by whom all things were made: who for us men and our salvation came down from heaven, and was incarnate by the Holy Ghost of the Virgin Mary. And was made man, and was crucified also for us under Pontius Pilate. He suffered and was buried, and the third day he rose again according to the Scriptures, and ascended into heaven, and sitteth on the right hand of the Father. And he shall come again with glory to judge both the quick and the dead: whose kingdom shall have no end.

And I believe in the Holy Ghost, the Lord and giver of life, who proceedeth from the Father, who with the Father and Son together is worshipped and glorified, who spake by the prophets. And I believe one Catholic and Apostolic Church. I acknowledge one baptism for the remission of sins. And I look for the resurrection of the dead, and the life of the world to come.

Technically speaking not much hangs on the differences between these classical expressions of the Christian intellectual heritage. What matters in the present context is that one of them be handed over to be received by those joining the church and entering into the kingdom of God. The reasons for this proposal are both positive and negative.

To begin, the Christian starting out on the journey of faith needs a good, meaty summary of the Christian faith. He or she needs an overview of the Christian worldview. This the classical creeds of the church provides. This is no accident, for the early creeds were developed for use in the context of Christian baptism. They enabled the young Christian to grasp the fundamental intellectual structure of the Christian mind, distinguishing it from the many options which were available in the marketplace of ideas in the ancient world. In the modern world we face an intense competition for the hearts and minds of people. Those who join the Christian church deserve to have access to the mind of the church as that mind was formed and shaped in response to the mysterious action of God in history and in their midst.

Notice at this point how brief the creeds are. They can be written on a postcard. They are not a vast, complicated theological treatise. They avoid as far as possible a heavy use of technical, philosophical or theological jargon. They focus on what God has done in Jesus Christ in the inauguration of the rule of God on earth. They express what the early Christians were driven to say when they thought through the intellectual consequences of the coming of the kingdom of God in Jesus Christ. Over the years they have stood the test of time, and they clearly embody what the church as a whole has found essential to its existence over the long haul of history.

On the negative side, the alternatives to the classical creeds of the church are not very alluring. Some would prefer to let the young Christian work out everything from scratch on their own. This is just unrealistic. People will informally turn to their favourite television evangelist or whoever else is close at hand and adopt what they have to offer as a substitute. Moreover, the faith of the church is not the product of our private theological endeavours. It is the work of the whole church as embodied in its intellectual tradition.

Others will seek to make a doctrine of scripture or a short list of basic fundamentals the alternative to the classical creeds of the church. This is especially popular in fundamentalist circles or among so-called nondenominational churches and movements. This is deeply flawed because the theory of scripture or the list of fundamentals generally provided is the product of sectarian movements within modern Protestantism rather than anything catholic or ecumenical in scope and content. More importantly, this provides the wrong kind of creed because its centre is not in God, in Jesus Christ, and in the Holy Spirit, but in some complicated account of the origin of the bible. As Methodists we stand in the mainstream of the classical Christian intellectual tradition and it is therefore fitting than we hand on its central symbols of faith to future generations rather than a sectarian rendering of the Christian heritage.

In handing over the creed it is important to bear the following general points in mind.

1. The creed was never meant to be exhaustive of the Christian intellectual heritage. On the one hand, the church has always insisted that no form of words adequately captures the truth about God and God's work in salvation. On the other hand, it has recognised that the creed is part of a wider body of tradition expressed in continuous theological reflection within the Christian community. Hence the creed is never taken as the exclusive and last word in Christian doctrine. It is, however, the first word, and it provides an irreducible core of Christian teaching.

2. Alongside the creed the church hands over the holy scriptures as norm and fountainhead of its teaching. In doing so it hands over a vast array of material which acts as a kind of indispensable road map to help one grow in grace and to find one's way to the promised land. In developing a canon of scripture the church never intended this canon to be taken alone. The church also put together its creeds to act as vital summary of the fundamental meaning of the action of God laid out in the scriptures. Scripture and creed, therefore, belong together; they are to be received and handed on as precious gifts of God to the Christian community.

3. In the reception of the creed what matters is less the understanding of all its content than an appreciation of the creed as the intellectual manifesto and bedrock of the Christian community. Understanding and adopting the creed as the foundation of one's life and thought is an ongoing process. This is why it is recited so often in the liturgy and why its content shows up again and again in the hymns of the church.

What is at stake here is a grasp of the intellectual content of the Christian tradition together with a readiness to allow the Holy Spirit to heal and redeem one's mind. Anti-intellectualism has no place in the Christian community. This takes bizarre forms at times. It can take the form of an opposition to all creeds as a barrier to intellectual freedom. This ultimately leads to intellectual chaos and confusion. Or it can take the form of a dogmatic fundamentalism which has no room for tradition in the life of the mind. This leads to a narrowing of the Christian vision and the adoption of a sectarian mindset as the hallmark of the Christian intellect. Methodists for good or ill have chosen to travel the main road of Christian history; it is essential that its members over the generations be given a chance to make that same journey. Receiving the classical creeds of the church is the first step in our travels on the main road.

SPIRITUAL GIFTS

In entering into the kingdom of God one enters into an experience of the Holy Spirit at a spiritual level which is comparable to one's immersion in water at a physical level. John the Baptist prophesied this when he declared that he baptised in water but the coming Messiah would baptise people with the Holy Spirit and with fire [Luke 3:16]. This is an extremely important dimension of one's initiation into the reign of God. If we fail to deal with this matter, Christians will be deprived of a vital source of grace and power both in their daily lives and in their ministries within the church.

There is no doubt but that there is a clear link between the coming of the Holy Spirit at Pentecost and the dawning of the new age of the reign of God. One of the hallmarks of the presence of the kingdom is the manifestations of the power of the Holy Spirit. This is evident in the ministry of Jesus. His miracles, his acts of exorcism, his acts of healing, his astonishing discernment, and his prophetic insight and rhetoric display in dramatic form the presence of the Holy Spirit in his life and work. That same power is manifest in the lives of the early disciples at Pentecost and thereafter. Their speaking in tongues, their boldness in preaching the gospel, their miracles, acts of healing, and exorcisms, and their prophetic insight show that they were experiencing the same unseen power of the Holy Spirit which was active in the ministry of Jesus.

Modern Christians have been at a loss to know what to do with this dimension of the presence of the kingdom of God. Some are embarrassed by their presence in the scriptures and in the history of the church. Some argue that they had only a limited function in the history of the church so that they ceased to exist at some point between the end of the first and fourth centuries. Some accept the possibility of these phenomena but treat them as the extraordinary work of the Holy Spirit and see them therefore as marginal and abnormal. Some dismiss this material as legend and myth, treating it as the product of a first-century, unscientific mindset.

In my view none of these alternatives are satisfactory. I agree entirely with Wesley that these manifestations of the Holy Spirit were given to the church for all time. It is obvious from a careful study of the history that they never entirely died out. They cease to exist because of our unbelief or our scepticism. When we seek the fulness of the reign of God in our midst they become a normal part of Christian ministry. Hence, they occur again and again in the history of religious awakenings and revivals, and they currently crop up in the Third World among those Christians who are not encumbered with Western scepticism.

In other words when the people of God seek for and enter into a fresh outpouring of the Holy Spirit, the Holy Spirit invariably seeks to make available resources in ministry which go far beyond the mere cultivation of our natural gifts and talents. As we are immersed, baptised, and filled with the Holy Spirit, we experience the dynamic and varied manifestations of the Holy Spirit in the church and in our work for Christ in the world. Entering naturally and without fuss or emotionalism into the full workings of the Holy Spirit is the birthright of every person who enters into the reign of God inaugurated by Jesus Christ.

Theological disputes as to how best to understand the exact working of the Holy Spirit in our lives are a secondary affair. Thus many follow Wesley in suggesting that many Christians experience a gap between their experience of assurance and forgiveness and their experience of other aspects of the work of the Holy Spirit. There is merit in this perspective for it generally does take time for us to come to terms with all that God wants to do in our lives. Yet Wesley was reluctant to set a rigid pattern for everybody, and he refused to be dogmatic about the timing of the work of the Holy Spirit. What matters is that we realise that in the end Christians receive only one gift, namely, the gift of the Holy Spirit, while the working out of the full implications of receiving the Holy Spirit is a process which cannot be forced on people.

As we pursue this issue in the context of initiation, it is helpful to bear the following considerations in mind.

1. The crux of the matter is the point that Christians are commissioned by their baptism to participate in the general ministry of the church and that they are given the Holy Spirit to fulfil that role in the church and the world. Those entering the kingdom need to own this with gratitude. They are appointed to be agents of God's kingdom; they are not meant simply to sit in pews and listen to sermons; they are called to the complex and varied ministry of the risen Christ through his body, the church.

2. Specific instruction should be given on the manifestations of the Holy Spirit as laid out in the relevant biblical passages such as Romans 12, I Corinthians 12-14, and Ephesians 4. This can be tied in with relevant teaching on the person of the Holy Spirit and on the work of the Holy Spirit in the church and the world.

3. It is helpful to organise workshops or training sessions which would help those being initiated to discern and work with the manifestations of the Holy Spirit. Initially this may appear somewhat threatening to some people but there is no substitute for firsthand experience initially as an observer and then as a participant.

4. It is only to be expected that people will have difficulty at times in coming to terms with this

aspect of initiation into the reign of God. It may take a full generation or more for the modern church to understand and accept what has until recently been dismissed as peripheral and strange. Even those most experienced in this dimension of the presence of the kingdom have much to learn. Many theologians have not yet caught up with the fresh winds of the Spirit blowing in the church universal. Yet it is vital that the church retrieve the fulness of the work of the Holy Spirit and that this be passed on to coming generations of Christians. There are ultimately no good excuses for inactivity in this area.

SPIRITUAL DISCIPLINES

It is very easy to go off the rails in one's spiritual life. As long as they live, Christians of every degree of maturity and understanding face assault from the world, the flesh, and the devil. For this reason the church provides an array of spiritual disciplines which provide nourishment, strength, and resources for coping with evil. Where these are neglected, Christians will falter and fall into sin. It is imperative that those entering the kingdom of God receive these disciplines and learn to use them effectively.

Wesley referred to these disciplines as means of grace. He understood them to be regular or ordinary channels which God uses to convey his grace to the souls of men and women. He held the chief of these means to be prayer, whether in secret or with the great congregation, searching the scriptures (which for Wesley implied reading, hearing, and meditating thereon), and receiving the Lord's Supper, eating bread and drinking wine in remembrance of Christ. In insisting on the use of means of grace, Wesley was rejecting the proposals of those who looked on outward forms as mere decoration or even as harmful to one's spiritual life. Wesley, of course, argued vehemently that the means of grace must be approached in the right way and with the right spirit, but this in no way slackened his conviction about their positive role in nourishing the life of faith.

Methodists have followed Wesley in this regard. In fact this is how they got their name for the term "Methodist" was simply a tag attached to them because they were so methodical about their attendance on the means of grace. Over the years they have cultivated the classical spiritual disciplines with enthusiasm. Originally it was the custom for all preachers to fast on Wednesday and Friday until about 3.00 p.m. In modern times the list of disciplines which Wesley used has expanded to include the whole range of disciplines to be found in the church universal. This is a very healthy development, although we should be careful not to neglect the basic disciplines such as fasting, prayer, scripture study, and attendance at the eucharist. It is better to gain mastery over the fundamental disciplines rather than dabble superficially in a host of them.

Applied to the context of initiation, it is useful to consider the following points.

1. Although instruction which covers the whole range of spiritual disciplines should be provided, it is best to concentrate on the fundamental disciplines of prayer, fasting, scripture study, and attendance at the eucharist. There is plenty of time over the long haul of one's spiritual journey to learn how to use all the disciplines. At the beginning it is best to concentrate on a few of the disciplines and deal thoroughly with them.

2. It is advisable to develop some way to build accountability into the actual practice of the spiritual disciplines. It is clearly not enough just to know what the disciplines are and why they are important. It is vital that the initiate learn to pray, to fast, to read the scriptures, and the like. This needs time and feedback from the personal experience of the learner if it is to be effective. There is a place here for the use of well planned small groups. It is especially fortunate for the person being initiated if he or she can find a good spiritual director to get one established in the use of the disciplines.

3. It is important to stress once again that entry into the kingdom is not earned by one's use of the

spiritual disciplines. One gains entry to the kingdom purely and solely through grace and mercy. Nor does mastery of the spiritual disciplines make one into some kind of superior Christian who can look down on others. The spiritual disciplines are simply channels of God's grace given to us as a bulwark against temptation, sin, foolishness, and nonsense. They are to be used solely as a means of seeking God and of developing our relationship with him.

CONCLUSION

Over the last two chapters we have explored what is involved in becoming grounded in the rule of God. The goal of this process is not to impose a set of heavy burdens on those who come to Christ. Nor is it at all the intention to exclude anyone from the kingdom. The aim is to be faithful to the meaning of the inauguration of God's kingdom as that is manifested and worked out in history. The dimensions I have identified cannot be ignored if we are to do even minimal justice to the coming of the reign of God in our midst. If we neglect these in our evangelism then our ministry will be hopelessly incomplete. Moreover, we shall have stored up trouble for ourselves and for those we have sought to introduce to the riches of Christ.

What is also at stake is a genuine balance in our spiritual lives. Too much evangelism results in spiritual abortions, or it fosters the development of crippled Christians who fall far short of the privileges and responsibilities given to us in the kingdom. Think of it this way. If we insist, say, only on new birth and conversion, we shall have Christians who are born again but who are morally weak, anti-intellectual, and ineffective in ministry. If we insist, say, only on belief in the creeds, we shall have Christians who are intellectually alert but spiritually dead. If we insist, say, only on baptism and the use of spiritual disciplines, we shall have Christians who are outwardly religious but inwardly unsure of their salvation and intellectually confused. If we insist, say, only on spiritual gifts, we shall have activist Christians who are lacking in understanding and love. If we insist, say, only on the adoption of Christian morality, we shall have Christians who are morally upright and pharisaical but spiritually blind and intellectually malformed.

Those seeking to enter into the kingdom of God deserve to have access to the full riches of the gospel. As we seek to put in place a ministry of evangelism which embraces this, we shall be developing the heritage of Methodists in a way which creatively builds on our quest for Christian perfection.

If this is to be done properly it will eventually mean that we shall have to establish the catechumenate again in the life of the church. The catechumenate was originally a process of instruction which was required of all those entering into the church. As Christianity spread into Gentile territory, it became essential to have a time for converts to assimilate the basics of Christianity. Sensitively and prudently employed, such an institution could deal in a comprehensive way with the dimensions of initiation we have identified here.

BIBLIOGRAPHY:

William J. Abraham, The Logic of Evangelism (Grand Rapids: Eerdmans, 1989). chap. 6.

John Burnaby, The Belief of Christendom (London: S.P.C.K., 1959).

Karl Barth, Dogmatics in Outline (London: SCM, 1949).

Geoffrey Wainwright, Doxology (New York: Oxford University Press, 1980).

Thomas Oden, Doctrinal Standards in the Wesleyan Tradition (Grand Rapids: Francis Asbury Press, 1988).

John Wimber, Power Evangelism (San Francisco: Harper and Row, 1986).

-------- Power Healing (San Francisco: Harper and Row, 1988).

James D. G. Dunn, Baptism in the Holy Spirit (London: SCM, 1970).

George Mallone, Those Controversial Gifts (Downers Grove: InterVarsity Press, 1983).

Richard Foster,   Celebration of Discipline
          (San Francisco: Harper and Row, 1978).
John Wesley, "Cautions and Directions Given to the
Greatest Professors in the Methodist Societies,"
in Albert Outler, ed.,   John Wesley
(New York: Oxford University Press, 1964), pp. 298-305.
------ "The Duty of Constant Communion," pp.332-344.
------ "The Means of Grace," in Albert Outler, ed.,
The Works of John Wesley, I, Sermons, I, 1-33
          (Nashville: Abingdon Press, 1984), pp. 376-397.
Richard Lovelace,   Dynamics of Spiritual Life
                    (Exeter: Paternoster Press, 1979)

QUESTIONS:

1. How would you summarise the intellectual content of the Christian faith?

2. What is the place of the classical creeds in the life of the church today?

3. Why is a summary of the faith important to the beginning Christian?

4. How does the Holy Spirit equip people for ministry?

5. How can we best get across the idea of lay ministries to those joining the Christian community?

6. What are the means of grace? How many do you think there are? Are some spiritual disciplines more important than others?

7. What is the best way to give instruction to new converts about spiritual disciplines?

8. As you look over the last two chapters, set up an initiation process which would ground people in the six dimensions of initiation outlined above. Make sure you do justice to all the dimensions mentioned. Also, be versatile and creative in the time allotted, the means to be used, the leaders who will be needed, and the like. Consider how present forms of membership training, spiritual retreats, and currently used workshops might be incorporated into the process?

9. In the light of your discussion and reflection what concrete, specific steps should you take to implement your convictions in the ministry of evangelism in your church?

CHAPTER SEVEN

MOVING OUT IN EVANGELISM

A BRIEF REVIEW

As I mentioned at the beginning, my aim in developing this book is to help local congregations think through and implement a coherent and responsible vision of evangelism within their specific situations. We now need to stand back a moment and review the ground we have covered. We also need to say something about motivation in evangelism.

PROSPECTS FOR THE FUTURE

The prospects for renewal in the field of evangelism in the present generation are unusually high. As a result of its commitment to the Decade of Evangelism, the Methodist Church is well placed to become a vital force for evangelism in the future. Several considerations support this contention. First, there is widespread concern among us about the decline of the denomination. Some of this is undoubtedly self-serving and panicky; hence, there is an immediate tendency to adopt whatever strategy of church growth we can find close at hand to save the institution. However, my distinct impression is that Methodists will move beyond this natural reaction to the bad news about decline and seek, by the grace of God, to find something more than simply strategies to swell the numbers.

Secondly, the last General Conference made it clear that Methodism is eager to continue to retrieve the great intellectual themes and doctrines which not only gave it identity over the years but in part enabled it to become such an astonishing agent of evangelism in earlier generations. Authentic evangelism must be rooted in authentic Christian teaching about the gospel. It cannot survive in a theological vacuum, nor can it exist for long in communities which hang loose to their moorings in the classical faith of the church. At times Methodists have been incredibly ignorant of their own theological roots and identity. At other times they have fostered naive and romantic conceptions of their church as the bastion of unending theological reconstruction. As a theologian I cherish the freedom and creativity of our tradition, but I welcome the current concern manifest in many quarters to retrieve and renew our classical rendering of the Christian tradition. Without this we are destined to offer the world stones when they ask for bread.

So our first task was to pause and assess our prospects for service in the field of evangelism. My claim is that the resources are there and we should have the nerve to use them with flair and enthusiasm. Each local church needs to sit down and calmly weigh up its capacities in the field of evangelism. As it does this, it should remember that evangelism is a ministry which will only be effective if it is animated by the winds of the Holy Spirit. The Holy Spirit alone can supply the energy, inspiration, compassion, and vision which are essential to responsible forms of evangelism.

CLARIFYING THE OPTIONS

Another crucial dimension of our proposals is that we need to clarify our fundamental convictions about the nature of evangelism. The options we face are clear. We can, for example, focus on witness, on proclamation, or on church growth as the centre of our evangelistic ministry. Obviously, we can learn from those who have insisted on these themes as the heart of the matter. I hope that those who are committed to these alternatives will bring their insights and concerns to the body for assimilation and action. Yet I am convinced that the real issue is how we relate evangelism to the dawning of the reign of God. This was the primary horizon of the early church and it was absolutely fundamental to the ministry of Christ. I suggested, therefore, that the goal of evangelism should be the grounding of people in the dynamic rule of God, made possible by the activity of the Holy Spirit, and manifested and inaugurated in the life, death, and resurrection of Jesus Christ. This is a plausible way to understand the labours of our mothers and fathers in the Methodist tradition, and it is a fruitful way to conceive of evangelism for our contemporary situation.

THE IMPORTANCE OF INITIATION

Consequently, the key phrase to grasp is that of genuine initiation into the kingdom of God. We should look at evangelism as that set of actions which are governed by the intention to initiate people into the kingdom of God. Anything we do which falls within the boundary of this goal should be construed as evangelism. This can range all the way from a quiet conversation with a neighbour, to the loaning of a good book on the meaning of Christianity to a friend, to the delivery of a passionate plea to accept Jesus Christ as lord and saviour, to the instruction given to a confirmation class, and so on. Evangelism will therefore require of us creativity and dexterity. It is not a single act like blowing a kiss or signing a cheque. It is a varied set of activities like farming or teaching.

This is one reason why no single program in the local church can do justice to the demands laid upon us in evangelism. What is needed is a complex network of actions and programs which together constitute the ministry of evangelism in our midst. This is also why evangelism cannot be shunted off onto the shoulders of the pastor or of a few eager lay persons. It must be owned as the responsibility of the whole church. Every Christian has a role to play in initiating and sustaining the ministry of evangelism. To express this in biblical terms, every Christian is called to lend a hand in the fulfilling of the great commission given to the earliest apostles.

THE HEART OF THE GOSPEL

Essential to this process is the ability to sum up the gospel in an acceptable manner. D. L. Moody, for example, held to a simple summary which was pegged in this fashion. He believed in ruin by the fall, redemption by the blood of Christ, and regeneration by the Holy spirit. In Irish Methodism in the last generation we often referred to the essentials of the faith in this way. We believe that all have sinned, that all can be saved from their sins, that all can know themselves saved, and that all can be saved to the uttermost. Taken on their own and ripped from the wider fabric of Christian doctrine and tradition these summaries would be grossly misleading. However, rightly used they are crucial, for most people do not have the time or the desire to grasp a long theological treatise.

In developing our summaries of the gospel it is vital to be faithful to the heart of the message of the New Testament. This centres in the good news of the inauguration of the kingdom of God in the life, death and resurrection of Jesus Christ. In the end the gospel is Jesus Christ for he is nothing less than God incarnate present on earth. In him we see the rule of God manifest among us. By his death he has reconciled us to God, and by his resurrection he has shattered the powers of darkness. Through the Holy Spirit, he now acts to set at liberty the whole of creation and to establish a community to bear witness to the gospel.

THE IMPORTANCE OF FAITH SHARING

That evangelism is a multi-action ministry does not entail that we are unable to pick out certain actions as especially characteristic of those engaged in this vital ministry. Just as there are characteristic acts which farmers perform in their farming, so there are characteristic things which workers in evangelism do in their evangelism.

One characteristic element in evangelism is faith sharing. Evangelists, whether lay or ordained, will find themselves again and again sharing the good news of the kingdom of God with others. Hence we devoted a whole chapter to this.

Church members need to be able to talk with others about Jesus Christ and about what he has done for them and the whole creation. Initially this can be daunting and embarrassing, but if this is carried out first of all among friends and known believers, then it can easily be transferred to the networks of relationships to which we all belong. Moreover, those set apart for the ordained ministry of the church need to be able to present the fundamentals of the gospel with clarity, wit, and graciousness. This is a skill which can be fostered and developed, as it is watered by the anointing of the Holy Spirit. There is also a place in the economy of the church for the holding of preaching missions where the services are carefully geared to the winsome presentation of the gospel to those who are uncommitted. In fact all sorts of avenues should be explored to ensure that the gospel of the kingdom is being announced as regularly as the evening news.

METHOD IN EVANGELISM

Another set of activities which is integral to the initiation of people into the kingdom of God is intimately related to the six dimensions which are clearly identifiable once we begin to spell out what such initiation really means. It makes no sense to speak of initiation into the reign of God without dealing with conversion, baptism, the foundations of Christian morality, the classical creeds of the church, spiritual gifts, and spiritual disciplines. Those who have heard the good news of the kingdom and turn towards it in repentance and faith need to be taken through a process which will deal with these matters.

Conversion is important because it highlights the impact of the coming of the kingdom on our personal histories. Entry into the kingdom means that we can never be quite the same again. We are given the opportunity to start all over again.

Baptism is important because the kingdom is given to a specific community, namely, the church. We are called to enter into that community, and the port of entry is the sacrament of baptism. In order to ensure that those who are baptised as infants genuinely own the faith for themselves it is profitable to have confirmation as an additional rite of the church.

Christian morality is also important. The kingdom entails a particular moral structure which is splendidly summed up in the great commandment to love God and their neighbour. One cannot enter the kingdom and reject its moral traditions.

Likewise with the early creeds of the church. These sum up in a suitable fashion the fundamental intellectual content of the impact of the reign of God. The early Christians were rightly concerned to think through the implications of their experience of Christ and the Holy Spirit. We cannot sit loose to the intellectual moorings which they were inspired to establish as they developed the canon of scripture and as they set up forms of discipline in the community to safeguard the treasure of the gospel.

It is also important to attend to the workings of the Holy Spirit in the body. Christians are irreversibly called to be agents of the kingdom. To this end they need to find their place in the general ministry of the church and come to discern the manifestations of the Holy Spirit in their midst.

Finally, it is important that those entering the kingdom of God be given access to the traditions of spiritual discipline which have become enshrined in the classical means of grace. They should especially be instructed in the basics of prayer, fasting, bible study, and attendance at the eucharist.

It will take time for all this to be incorporated into a comprehensive network of experiences which forms a unitary process. My ultimate goal is to see the institution of the catechumenate established in an appropriate way in the modern church. It matters not a whit what we call what we do at this point. What is vital is that we find a way beyond mere proclamation and conversion to embrace a vision of evangelism which will be satisfied with nothing less than the incorporation of people into the reign of God on earth.

THE QUESTION OF MOTIVATION

It is appropriate at this stage to say something about motivation. It is not enough to have a vision; nor is it sufficient to establish all sorts of seminars, workshops, committees, and the like; we need to step out in faith and get on with the job.

Why should we do this? There are a multitude of reasons. Let me mention just four.

1.　The church needs to move out in evangelism because we are under orders from our risen Lord to take the gospel to the ends of the earth.

　　We can see this initially in the sending out of the twelve. They were told to go to the lost sheep of the house of Israel, to preach, saying that the kingdom of God was at hand, and in addition they were to heal the sick, raise the dead, cleanse the lepers, and cast out demons [Matt. 10:5-8]. The mission to Israel was a temporary assignment. After the resurrection, the apostles were told to go to all nations and make disciples. Each of the evangelists records the details of the great commission in his own way, but the whole thrust of the intention of Jesus is clear. The church is to take the gospel to the whole world, make disciples, and establish Christian communities [Matt. 28: 16-20]. In time this is exactly what they early church did, even though it initially took persecution to drive them out of Jerusalem and to take the gospel to the Gentile world.

To be sure, there are times in its history when the church has either abandoned its evangelistic responsibilities entirely, or it has become hostile to this aspect of its total ministry. On occasion evangelism has become a kind of underground activity carried on by disciples who have more zeal than they have knowledge. This in turn can breed further indifference within the main streams of the Christian tradition. Add to this our normal, human propensity for laziness, disobedience, timidity, fear, and selfishness, and we have perfectly adequate explanations for the church's failures in this arena. Yet the passion for evangelism has never completely died out. Thus the Methodist movement can be understood as a remarkable case study of the rekindling of the evangelistic ministry of the church. Against great odds, our forefathers and foremothers were impelled by the Holy Spirit to rediscover the gospel and to share it eagerly with all and sundry. Likewise today there are sections of the church which have refused to abandon this vital aspect of apostolic succession.

One of the key questions facing the Methodist Church in the next generation is whether it will once more rediscover its evangelistic responsibilities in the modern world. We can be sure of one thing: if it does not, then God will use others to find the lost sheep and bring them into his kingdom. Sometimes we like to ask the question: What can the Methodist Church do for God in our day and generation? The assumption is that we are in charge, and that we are in a place to decide what God ought to do in the ministry of his church. Perhaps it would be better to ask a different question: What will God do with the Methodist Church in the light of his intention to see all come to a knowledge of salvation? The prophet Ezekiel makes very clear what is in store for shepherds and sheep who enjoy the benefits of the covenant with God but who refuse to share in God's concern to reach out to others: God will set them aside and, if need be, he will get the job done some other way [Ezekiel 34].

2. The church needs to move out in evangelism because in doing so the church is itself constantly renewed in its faith and commitment.

This happens in a number of ways. To begin, there is something deeply refreshing in encountering again and again those who are converted to Christ and brought into the Christian community. There is a spontaneous joy and innocence in the beliefs and actions of the new convert which reminds more seasoned Christians of the beauty and wonder of the gospel. Secondly, in sharing the gospel with others the church returns in a regular way to those primordial events and practices in which is enshrined the heart and soul of the gospel. It can never forget the rock from which it was hewn and the bread by which it is constantly fed.

Thirdly, sharing the gospel with others fosters an interest in and interaction with the thought and life of each new generation. It is regularly challenged thereby to faithfulness in service within its specific context and setting. It cannot afford to be out of touch either with God or with those it is seeking to reach. Hence evangelism fosters a healthy dialogue between the church and the world and between past and present. It keeps the church alert, driving it back to its roots, yet doing this without permitting it to become antiquarian and self-satisfied.

3.   The church needs to move out in evangelism because in doing so it brings light and hope to a dark and chaotic world.

Our modern western societies are facing a profound crisis as they move into the future. The crowbar of events has smashed the romantic illusion that we can live without God and without the means of grace given to us in the Christian heritage. The spread of secularism over the last two centuries has not been the heaven on earth which was promised by those who argued that Christianity is obsolete and who piously believed that our welfare is to be found in our own devices and resources. The greed, violence, materialism, selfishness, and general nastiness which stalk the land is ample testimony that we cannot live without the gospel of Christ. The world was created to love and adore God and until it relearns this crucial lesson, its prospects are bleak in the extreme.

Further failure of nerve within the church in evangelism will be disastrous. The gospel offers light and hope to all who will repent and enter into the rule of God launched in and through Jesus Christ. Christians of all denominations need to join together in a concerted effort to retrieve the fulness of the gospel of the kingdom and to engage in forms of evangelism which will settle for nothing less that the dawning of the age to come in our midst.

The potential for such a recovery is genuine, but it is by no means secure. It will be utterly inadequate to settle for the fostering of the traditional forms of civil religion which are still so common among us. Nor will it do to rest content with the dregs of the revivals which have swept through the nation over the last hundred years or so. We need a fresh anointing of the Holy Spirit and a resolute and patient attempt to develop a ministry of evangelism which will do justice to all that God has done for the world in Jesus Christ. This is the minimum which we need to match the challenge of the hour.

4.   The church needs to move out in evangelism because in doing so God is glorified to the ends of the earth.

Our ultimate end as creatures of a good and loving Creator is to love God and enjoy him for ever. This does not sing well in a culture which measures everything by crude, materialistic yardsticks. Yet this is our true end, and within it we find our ultimate happiness and final destiny. As the gospel is preached and as people are prudently and lovingly brought into the kingdom of God, God is glorified and adored. We are told by our Lord that the angels rejoice when one sinner repents and returns to God. So in our evangelism we not only see heaven begin to come on earth, we also cause the courts of heaven to resound in praise and joy. Let us therefore go forth with boldness and confidence to magnify and glorify the mysterious Trinity.

Ye neighbours and friends of Jesus draw near:
His love condescends by titles so dear
To call and invite you his triumph to prove,
And freely delight you in Jesus's love.
The Shepherd who died His sheep to redeem;
On every side are gathered to Him,
The weary and burdened, the reprobate race;
And wait to be pardoned through Jesus's grace.
The blind are restored through Jesus's name;
They see their dear Lord, and follow the Lamb;
The halt they are walking, and running the race;
The dumb they are talking of Jesus's grace.

The deaf hear His voice and comforting word,
It bids them rejoice in Jesus their Lord:
Thy sins are forgiven, accepted thou art;
They listen, and heaven springs up in their heart.
The lepers from all their spots are made clean,
The dead by their call are raised from their sin;
In Jesu's compassion the sick find a cure,
And gospel salvation is preached to the poor.

They seek Him and find Him: they ask and receive
The Friend of mankind, who bids them believe:
On Jesus they venture, His gift they embrace,
And forcibly enter His kingdom of grace.
O Jesus, ride on till all are subdued,
Thy mercy made known, and sprinkle thy blood;
Display thy salvation, and teach the new song
To every nation, and people, and tongue.

BIBLIOGRAPHY;

Vincent J. Donovan,   Christianity Rediscovered, an
                      Epistle from the Massai
                              (Maryknoll: Orbis, 1978).
Donald A. McGavran,   Understanding Church Growth
                  (Grand Rapids: Eerdmans, 1980), Part One.
Orlando E. Costas,   Christ Outside the Gate
                              (Maryknoll: Orbis, 1982).
David Paton & Charles H. Long,
     A Roland Allen Reader: The Compulsion of the Spirit
              (Grand Rapids: Eerdmans, Cincinnati, 1983).
Michael Green,   Evangelism through the Local Church
                              (London: Hodder 1990).
G. Howard Mellor (ed),   The Good News Works
                              (London: Home Mission Division of the
                                  Methodist Church, 1992).

QUESTIONS:

1. Summarise the fundamental conclusions you have reached about the nature of evangelism as you complete your study of this manual.

2. If your were rewriting this book what changes would you make? Send a brief note detailing your suggestions to the author.

3. What motivates you to go out into the world and engage in evangelism?

4. Most congregations have some members who are uneasy with or hostile to evangelism. What can you do to win them over to a deep commitment to evangelism?

5. What can you do to foster a healthy ministry of evangelism at district and conference level?

6. Make a list of all that needs to be done to implement a comprehensive ministry of evangelism in your local church.

7. Outline the timeline and strategies you plan to adopt in order to accomplish the tasks laid out in answer to the last question.

APPENDICES

APPENDIX I
CONDUCTING A WORKSHOP
ON FAITH SHARING

It is very important that each local church have a core of believers who are able to share their faith without apology and without fuss. It would be wonderful if this were to happen spontaneously. Sometimes this is the case with certain individuals. They have the kind of contagious faith which spills over into a natural form of personal evangelism. As we know, however, this is the exception rather than the rule. So it is imperative that each church develop a workshop on faith sharing which is simple and effective.

Such a workshop can be developed by a local congregation if they set their mind to it. In what follows I lay out in a schematic form what they can do to put such a workshop in place.

Begin with a nucleus of people who are appointed to provide the leadership and overall direction to the project. Let them come together to take ownership of the planning and execution. Set a goal of organising a workshop in faith sharing. What will emerge may look something like this.

1. Hold initial meetings of the planning group to think through and plan the project.

2. Take time to spread the word in the congregation and then begin inviting anyone interested to sign up for the workshop. Do not be worried about either lack of interest or embarrassment. Proceed with quiet enthusiasm and hope.

3. Hold the first part of the workshop on a suitable evening. Sunday evening may be a convenient time.

    i. Have someone give an overview of the many ways in which Christians share their faith. The goal here is to show that Christians can share their faith in a host of ways. We will get to verbal sharing of the faith shortly; what matters initially is that people realise that they are already sharing their faith. What is going to happen is really an extension of that. This helps to put things in perspective.

The following ways of sharing the faith might be covered in the presentation:
a. Sharing the faith by one's life.
b. Sharing the faith by music and song.
c. Sharing the faith by giving good Christian literature to others.
d. Sharing the faith by supporting the work of the church in its varied ministry.
e. Sharing the faith by teaching a Sunday School class.
f. Sharing the faith by inviting a neighbour to church.

If need be, let the group divide into small groups and brain storm on the many ways in which the faith can be shared.

ii. Explain that one of the most powerful ways to share the faith is by word of mouth. Indicate why this is very important. This can be done by bringing out the limitations of other ways of sharing the faith and by identifying the advantages of the spoken word. This needs to be done thoroughly so that those listening are really convinced about this.

iii. Suggest that there are two distinct ways of tackling faith sharing by word of mouth. (a) Sharing the content of the gospel message with others. This is the more difficult and will be set aside for the moment. (b) Sharing the outline of one's own journey of faith to date. This will be the focus of the workshop.

iv. Now take up the issue of sharing one's own journey of faith. Indicate that these vary enormously. There is no right or wrong pattern to our spiritual journeys. Characteristically we can discern some common patterns which will help those present find a model to fit their experience. Indicate at this point very briefly the two patterns which shall be used.

Alternative patterns look like this:

Pattern A: What my life was like before I met Christ.
How I came to know about Christ.
How I met Christ.
What Christ means to me now.

Pattern B: What it was like to grow up in the faith from childhood.
The time in my life when I realised that Christ was crucial to me.
What Christ means to me now.

Draw attention to the fact that Pattern B is every bit as significant as Pattern A.

   v.   Let the person leading or presenting the material now take five minutes to share his or her journey of faith with the group.

   vi.   Finish by indicating that the aim of the workshop is to help the participants to share their faith with the rest of the group that is present. To that end distribute a sheet of paper giving instructions on how to share their faith with others. [Consult if need be for help at this point G Howard Mellor, The Good News Works, Papers 12 & 13.] Make sure that the instructions are clear. Provide a list of do's and dont's in the art of faith sharing. Also indicate some reading that they might find helpful between then and the next session. [See the bibliography at the end of chapter 4 above].

4.   Hold the second part of the workshop on another day, say, on Saturday morning.

   i.   Begin with appropriate singing, prayer, and devotions.

   ii.   Let the leader walk carefully through the possible patterns of faith which were mentioned towards the end of the last session. Stress again the importance of diversity. If possible use illustrations from autobiographies or testimonies which represent the patterns mentioned.

iii. Send everyone off alone with a piece of paper and a pen and invite them to jot down the main elements in their journey of faith. Fifteen to twenty minutes should suffice for this.

iv. On their return divide into small groups and let everyone have a chance to share their faith with the group. At the end of this let each group designate one person from their group to share their story with the whole body.

v. Take time to have the person selected from each group share their story again with the whole body. This can be a very emotional time so the leader must be ready to handle the situation sensitively.

vi. Discuss follow up together. You may want to have someone share their story with the whole congregation the following Sunday in the regular service. You may want to begin some monthly meetings where faith sharing is featured as the main event. You may want to set up a covenant group where the members report back on their experiences of faith sharing with others. This last option can be extraordinarily effective. I would urge the group to think this through and forge ahead with boldness. You may also want to organise another workshop which would focus this time on sharing the content of the gospel with others. Consult the reading in the bibliography for chapter 4 above on this.

vii. End with suitable singing and prayer.

HOW CAN I LEAD SOMEONE TO JESUS CHRIST?

Our training in evangelism is always incomplete if it fails to equip people to lead others to a personal commitment to Jesus Christ as lord and saviour. Every Christian should be able to lead an inquiring individual through those basic steps which enable him or her to put their trust in Christ for forgiveness and salvation.

Note that this is just one element in the ministry of evangelism.

Many people to whom we bring the gospel and whom we invite into the kingdom are not ready to make a commitment. We need to talk with them, share with them, listen to them, lend them some good literature, encourage them to seek God, answer their queries where we can, and so on. Coming to Christ is generally a process, so we need to give people time to understand and work things through. Moreover, after people have come to Christ, our work as evangelists is not complete until they are firmly grounded in the reign of God.

It is useful to think of the total process as a kind of scale stretching from unbelief to full commitment.

Hostility - Interest - Intellectual - Conversion - Membership

Unbelief - Attraction - Assent - in the Kingdom

In the light of this, success in evangelism is to be measured not by the number of people that we lead to Christ but by our ability to help people move along the journey from unbelief to unbelief. Thus it is a great achievement if we have managed, for example, to get a hostile and hurt unbeliever to consider seriously the possibility that Christianity might be true or or that God really loves him or her as an individual. Once we think of evangelism in this fashion we are released from anxiety and hastiness in our personal contacts with others.

As we examine this process, it is important to observe that people do ripen and come to a point where it is vital to present the challenge of personal commitment. Wesley suggested this when he divided people into various groups which melted into each other in real life. Thus, he spoke of the natural person who is indifferent and dead to the things of God. They may believe in God but they do not care a whit about their salvation. Then he identified the legal person. This is someone who is aware of sin and takes the issue of his or her standing before God very seriously, but he or she attempts to get right with God by a treadmill of religious and moral acts. Then there is the awakened person. This is the person who is aware of sin, but who despairs of forgiveness and salvation.

It is this person that is clearly the most ripe to be challenged by the good news, say, of forgiveness and assurance. In the light of all this, it would be idle and insensitive to march in and call for commitment to Christ without attending to the differences in these situations.

In the end there does come a time, however, when we must be ready to lead someone to Christ. If we are not able to do this properly we shall ultimately fail in our endeavours. I recall vividly a pastoral situation which highlights this. I had visited an old widower for months and had got nowhere in either sharing the gospel or talking to him about Christ. Then one afternoon I arrived on a pastoral call to be welcomed with enthusiasm. I quickly discovered that he had found Christ for himself. What had happened was this. A young woman close by had befriended this man on the death of his wife. Each day she cooked his dinner and brought it to him without complaint. When this did not stop but continued month after month, he could stand it no longer. He insisted that she tell him the secret of her love, and when she told him it was due to her being a Christian, he insisted on coming to the Christ that had inspired this kindness. Fortunately, the woman concerned was able to instruct him there and then, and was, moreover, able to lead him herself to Christ without fuss or embarrassment.

There is no absolutely right or wrong way to do this. Here is one way to tackle the issue.

1. Arrange or find a place where you will have privacy to talk to the person who is concerned to come to Christ. Begin privately with a simple prayer for God's help.

2. Put the person at ease. Be natural and conversational in your speech.

3. Ascertain if the person really does want to become a Christian. Look for seriousness and conviction at this point. Mere curiosity about the possibility of becoming a Christian is not enough at this point. If need be, ask straight out if the person would like to receive Christ as their saviour and follow him as their Lord.

4. Make sure that the person understands the content of the gospel. Work in your mind from a clear outline of the fundamental facts of sin, the work of Christ on the cross for our salvation, the need for repentance, and the cost of discipleship. Make clear that entry into the kingdom is a many-sided affair which will entail changes along the lines sketched out in the six dimensions of initiation.

5. Never press for a decision, although there is room for exhortation and encouragement. Trust the Holy Spirit to take the gospel and reveal its relevance and truth to the individual.

6. When the person is ready to say 'yes', suggest that they pray for the forgiveness of their sins, that they verbally invite Christ to be their saviour and lord, and that they surrender themselves to Christ. Do not be afraid to get on your knees to do this, and ensure that the prayer is loud and clear.

Where the person is reserved and is reticent to pray in his or her own words, do not hesitate to lead in a short prayer, which is repeated clause by clause. The following is a possibility: "Lord God Almighty, I confess that I am a sinner, deserving only your judgement. I thank you for providing for a Saviour in Jesus Christ your Son. I here and now acknowledge my need of Him. I repent of all my sins and I receive him as my personal Saviour and

Lord. I thank you for inviting me into your kingdom and I give myself unreservedly to live under your rule on earth. Help me henceforth. Amen."

7. Pray with the new convert, commending him or her to God and his mercy.

8. Deal immediately with the issue of assurance. Converts invariably look to their feelings to change in conversion. Divert this possibility by having them apply one of the great promises or affirmations of the gospel to their lives. Use John 3: 36, for example. Or use Rom. 10: 9-13. Make it absolutely clear that the passage applies to what they have done there and then. Explain that their feelings are not the issue and that the Holy Spirit will in God's good time give them an inner and additional testimony to their standing before God.

9. Suggest that the new convert share what has happened with another person who will be pleased to hear the news. They can do this by personal conversation face to face, by a phone call, by a letter, or whatever.

10. You will have already explained that accepting Christ as one's saviour and lord is part of a process which involves baptism and confirmation, instruction in the creed, learning to minister in the body, and so on. Now link the person into that process and see to it that their initiation into the kingdom is genuine rather than superficial.

ESTABLISHING A CATECHUMENATE

A crucial part of our work in evangelism is the process whereby the new believer is grounded in the basics of the Christian life in the kingdom of God. In my judgement this should be considered as an integral part of evangelism rather than something added on to evangelism. This is one area where the church as a whole is extremely weak so that it may take a generation to puts things right.

It is very important to walk patiently and prudently in this area. Some congregations may not be ready to take this on board. No good is served by barging ahead without the support and backing of the local congregation. Initially it may be best to proceed on a voluntary basis. The reason for this is that many Christians have never been adequately instructed in the six dimensions we identified as essential to serious initiation into the kingdom of God. Many current church members would benefit enormously from a process which would take them through a course designed for those entering the catechumenate. The ultimate dream would be for a whole congregation to decide to go through this process and then agree that all its new members should enter the church by initially joining the catechumenate.

Originally the catechumenate was the process which new Christians went through in order to participate in the full life of the local Christian congregation. Sometimes it took up to two years for this to be completed. It reached its climax in the service of baptism which was held on the eve of Easter Sunday. The reasons why this developed were varied, but the fundamental issue was the need for Christians coming out of paganism to be instructed in the fundamentals of the faith. After Christianity became the established religion of the Roman empire, the pressure to yield to quick and easy methods of initiation became so great that the process was eventually eroded beyond repair. In a sense it is impossible to restore the exact form of the catechumenate which was originally developed. But this is not the issue. What is at stake is our seriousness about instructing people in the Christian faith. Our current policy is haphazard and disastrous. We have reached the appalling point where the Christianity of the church in the West is intellectually thin and spiritually superficial. We are scarcely in a position to evangelise the culture due to the ignorance which abounds in our midst. Someday this is going to have to be tackled if we are to achieve the potential which we have in evangelism.

1. How might we proceed?
   We might usefully begin by reviewing our current ways of bringing people into church membership. Let a group in the church sit down and specify what it takes to become a member of their local congregation.

Examine what happens in the practice of baptism. Is this a genuine sacrament of entry into the church? Is it allowed to degenerate into a private, folksy, family affair, divorced from the church and the kingdom of God? Is it rushed through in a few minutes on a Sunday morning? Does the congregation own its responsibilities with the parents for the spiritual nurture of the child?

Then look at confirmation or its equivalent? Are those confirmed given the freedom not to join the church? If they join, do they know the faith into which they have been baptised? Is confirmation a kind of passing out parade from life in the local congregation so that its subjects are never seen again?

What is done with transfer members from other congregations? Is the process of transfer a matter of form only, so that no questions are asked about personal faith and commitment? Are those transferred genuinely welcomed into the body? Are they given an opportunity to share in the general ministry of the church?

What happens to those who join the church from the world? Are they given the chance to understand what they are doing? Are they instructed in the gospel? Are they received with gladness into the body?

We have to begin from where we are, so conduct a thorough review of what is involved in coming into membership of your local church. Do so without entering into judgement on anyone or on what is currently the case. Be loving and realistic. Make a serious evaluation determining as best you can how far the various groups entering the church through baptism, confirmation, transfer, and so on have a genuine chance of being grounded in the kingdom of God. Ask where and to what extend the six dimensions of initiation are covered in the current situation. I suspect that you will find that there is a need to establish a catechumenate course which will do remedial work among current church members and provide a useful preparation class for new members.

2. What might the catechumenate course look like?
I can envisage a course lasting up to six months. It would involve traditional learning sessions, retreats, workshops, and any other innovative strategies which would be useful in grounding people in the reign of God.

It could begin with a rite of entry. In this those concerned would covenant to seek the coming of the reign of God in their lives. This would be a time of joy and initial commitment.

It would then proceed with a series of classes on a variety of topics. Here are some possibilities.

Session i.	The Coming of the Rule of God.
Session ii.	The inauguration of the Kingdom in Jesus Christ.
Session iii.	Entry into the kingdom of God.
Session iv.	Conversion.
Session v.	Baptism and confirmation.
Session vi.	The Rule of Faith: The Nicene Creed.
Session vii.	The Rule of Life: The Great Commandment.
Session viii.	The work of the Holy Spirit in Ministry.
Session ix.	Spiritual disciplines.
Session x.	Review and summary.

Related to these sessions there would be a number of retreats and workshops designed to introduce the catechumen to the practical and experiential side of what is covered in the teaching sessions. Particular attention should be given to the work of the Holy Spirit and to the spiritual disciplines. It would be useful to have the catechumen identify the gifts and talents they wish to use in the body; and it would be equally important to begin using the central spiritual disciplines. It might be extremely helpful to include participation in a Walk to Emmaus as an essential part of the whole experience. Details of this can be obtained from the Home Mission Division or the Rev Howard Mellor at Cliff College.

The climax of the whole experience would be a service of commitment using the classical Methodist Covenant Service as the appropriate liturgy. This will probably need a special session beforehand devoted to preparation for the service.

The service itself should be a festive occasion. A place should be found for the laying on of hands and for other rites deemed helpful. A place should also be found to hand over a bible, a copy of the Nicene Creed, a copy of the General Rules of the Methodist Societies, a copy of some of John Wesley's sermons [Albert Outler, ed., John Wesley (New York: Oxford University Press, 1964) would be a suitable gift], and a certificate of Membership of the local Methodist church.

3. Final Comments.
   i.   There is value to having sponsors for those entering into the catechumenate. Their role is to be that of a friend and encourager to those going through the process.
   ii. It would be very helpful if you could make use of spiritual directors from within the congregation to lead individuals into a regular use of the spiritual disciplines. The spiritual directors do not need to be spiritual giants or experts; it is enough if they can clearly and in a friendly manner introduce the beginner to the basic means of grace.

iii.   It is possible to put the institution of the catechumenate in place initially on a voluntary basis. Simply develop the full course outlined above as a regular offering in the church. In time decisions can be made as to where to go from there.

iv.   Do not be surprised if there is resistance in certain quarters. Be ready to deal with objections and obstacles. Strong leadership will be needed to carry this kind of project through to completion.

v.   Note that the catechumenate as envisioned here would have a definite beginning and end. It is not intended to be a substitute for the continuing nurture and education which Christians need throughout their lives.

APPENDIX IV

MISCELLANEOUS SUGGESTIONS

1. Develop a small library of books which will be available in the church on the subject of evangelism. On appropriate occasions have someone bring a brief report on material that has been found useful. Intellectual laziness and indifference can kill evangelism; explore ways to foster stimulating reflection on evangelism.

2. Many people have strong emotions about evangelism. Evangelism has a bad image in our culture and in our church. People have been hurt in their past experience of evangelism. Appoint a group to come up with ways to help the church work through its negative experiences and to come to a positive feeling towards evangelism.

3. Contact the Wycliffe Bible translators, Home Mission Division or some other such group to help your church identify a group of people who have never yet heard of Jesus Christ. Explore what your local church can do to bring the gospel to them.

4. Set up a group to go through the book of Acts and examine the evangelistic activity portrayed by Luke. Find a way to share their findings with the whole church.

5. Engage someone to deliver a lecture in your church on the life and work of E Stanley Jones, Samuel Chadwick or William Sangster as an evangelist. Explore the possibility of engaging other lecturers to cover the lives of other evangelists, especially within the Wesleyan tradition.

6. Set up a task force to identify the different groups who are within reach of your church. Ask them to propose some specific ways in which these various groups might be reached with the gospel.

7. Set up a group to examine the growth or decline patterns in your church over the years. All the data you need to gather is identified in Bob Waymire and C. Peter Wagner, <u>The Church Growth Survey Book</u>. This can be obtained from Global Church Growth, Overseas Crusades, 25 Corning Avenue, Milpitas, CA 95035. Available through the Cliff College Bookshop, price on request.

8. Plan a short preaching mission in your church.

Useful Addresses

The Methodist Church Home Mission Division, 1 Central Buildings, Westminster, London, SW1H 9NH.

Cliff College, Calver, Sheffield, S30 1XG.

Quadrant (formerly Marc Europe) - Peter Brierley